GREEN DAY

First published in Great Britain in 2005
by Artnik
341b Queenstown Road
London SW8 4LH
UK

© *Alex Hannaford 2005*

ISBN 1–903906–72–5

Design: Supriya Sahai
Pictures: Live Photography
Book Concept: Nicholas Artsrunik
Editor: John McVicar

Printed and bound in Spain by Gráficas Díaz

GREEN DAY

ALEX HANNAFORD

ACKNOWLEDGEMENTS

This is, I believe, the first ever
Green Day book. If I'm wrong
I apologise. Either way, it wouldn't
have been possible without the
source material gleaned from the
list of publications & websites
below. To them I'm incredibly
grateful.

Chicago Tribune
The Sun
The Guardian
Los Angeles Times / Calendar
section
New Musical Express
Glasgow Herald
Glasgow Evening Times
Coventry Evening Telegraph
Evening Standard
Independent
Independent on Sunday
Washington Post
Western Daily Press
The Times
South Wales Echo
Rolling Stone
MTV
BBC
Greenday.com
Greenday.net
Greenday.org
Lookoutrecords.com
Greendayauthority.com
Geekstinkbreath.net
Rockonthenet.com
Ubl.com
allmusic.com

Thanks:
The staff of the British
Library (newspapers) at
Colindale: always helpful; the
café opposite for a brief
respite.

Court, mum, dad, Liz,
Valentina and, especially, Lucky,
Artnik's Golden Retriever.
And not least Supriya for framing my
text so brilliantly.

When Johnny Ramone died in his sleep in September 2004, the music world mourned the passing of a legend.

His band 'The Ramones' three minute blasts of infectious punk rock set the benchmark by which generations of future bands would be judged. The *Los Angeles Times* summed up their importance back in 1999: 'The Ramones invented punk-rock, the Sex Pistols put it on the map and the Clash left us its legacy… that's worth remembering as it becomes more and more obvious that punk is not going away. Decades after its big bang, the music continues to provide a resonant musical and lyrical vocabulary to restless youth.' Johnny Ramone pioneered punk's four chord simplicity – the 'anyone can play guitar' shtick – and his fast, repetitive style influenced pretty much every punk guitarist that sweated and spat their way around grimy stages across the world in his wake.

One particular guitar player he would inspire, Billie Joe Armstrong, had just turned two years old when the Ramones took to the stage in Queens, New York for their first ever gig back in March 1974.

'PUNK IS NOT JUST THE SOUND, THE MUSIC. PUNK IS A LIFE—STYLE.'
— BILLIE JOE ARMSTRONG

Fast forward 27 years and it's a hot June night in Washington DC. A small 12-year-old kid named Zack is in the mosh pit near the front of the stage. It's a sweating, seething mass of teenagers but he's having the time of his life.

Half way through the show, the singer starts to fish kids from the audience to replace the band on stage. **'WHO HERE CAN PLAY DRUMS.'** he bellows into the mike. A timid Zach sticks his hand in the air and catches the singer's eye immediately.

Within seconds he's hoisted on to the huge stage, a pair of drum sticks foisted into his sweaty palms and told to play. Slowly he begins to find his groove as the singer recruits two more people from the sweaty mosh pit below. A bassist; a guitarist and the line-up is complete.

The point being made that summer evening in Washington DC was that anyone could pull it off; anyone could play punk rock. The bleach-blonde haired man wearing black drainpipe trousers, silver choker and guitar pick around his neck, and pulling facial contortions who was modestly making the point was Billie Joe Armstrong. And the band he had just 'replaced' on stage with excited fans was Green Day. The punk rock, DIY ethic that had so inspired Billie Joe all those years ago was still alive and well.

But it's the underlying point to every two-hour eruption of molten music that is a Green Day

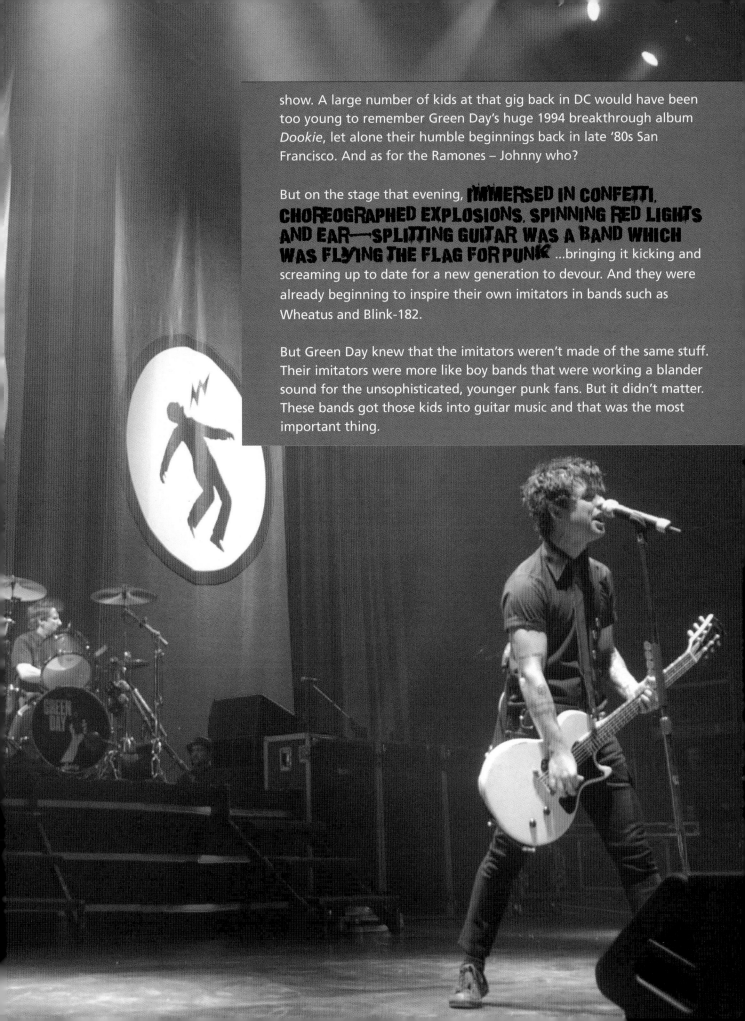

show. A large number of kids at that gig back in DC would have been too young to remember Green Day's huge 1994 breakthrough album *Dookie*, let alone their humble beginnings back in late '80s San Francisco. And as for the Ramones – Johnny who?

But on the stage that evening, IMMERSED IN CONFETTI, CHOREOGRAPHED EXPLOSIONS, SPINNING RED LIGHTS AND EAR—SPLITTING GUITAR WAS A BAND WHICH WAS FLYING THE FLAG FOR PUNK ...bringing it kicking and screaming up to date for a new generation to devour. And they were already beginning to inspire their own imitators in bands such as Wheatus and Blink-182.

But Green Day knew that the imitators weren't made of the same stuff. Their imitators were more like boy bands that were working a blander sound for the unsophisticated, younger punk fans. But it didn't matter. These bands got those kids into guitar music and that was the most important thing.

For Green Day, then, as now, it wasn't just about songs chronicling teenage boredom, sex and immaturity. 'Punk is not just about the music,' Billie Joe said at the time. 'Punk is a life-style. It's not about popularity and all that crap.' But popular was something Billie Joe's band just couldn't escape becoming.

GREEN DAY'S STORY BEGAN IN 1972.

In the US the Watergate scandal was rocking Nixon's White House; the California Supreme Court had claimed the state's death penalty was invalid and commuted the sentences of all death row inmates to life in prison; and *The Streets of San Francisco* – a new detective series starring a young Michael Douglas – had become the hottest thing on television. Elsewhere, in Rodeo, near the Bay Area of the city, Billie Joe Armstrong was born on February 17th.

Rodeo, California, is fifteen miles from Berkeley – a predominantly white, middle-class area just a short drive from San Francisco and home to the oldest college of the University of California. UC Berkeley dates back to the Gold Rush days of the 1840s.

Billie Joe may have lived in a relatively nice neighbourhood but he was from a working-class family. His father was a truck driver and jazz musician and his mother was a waitress at local restaurant, Rod's Hickory Pit, in Vallejo, where she 'slung hash' – a colloquialism for frying chopped meat and potatoes with spices. Vallejo was the original home of California's state government, but now it's known chiefly as the home of Six Flags Marine World theme park or for its downtown farmer's market. Billie Joe's mum was a hard worker but was used to the graft: she had slogged it out in hot kitchens as a waitress since she was 16 years old. Billie Joe was the youngest of six children and his mother had turned 40 by the time she gave birth to him. His father died of lung cancer when he was just 10 years old and Billie Joe became the typical latchkey kid. His mother was liberal in her attitude to raising children and would let him and his five siblings play in the street.

The year before his father died, Billie Joe had been given his first guitar: a blue Fernandes Stratocaster – a copy of a Fender, the choice guitar of musicians such as Jimi Hendrix and Stevie Ray Vaughn. He picked up an old 1959, 100 watt Marshall amp and he was all set.

IT'S NOT ABOUT POPULARITY AND ALL THAT CRAP

Rodeo was the type of town where playing the guitar could be your only ticket out, so it made sense that Billie Joe played until his fingers ached. To this day, he still plays the same Stratocaster... everyday.

Now with a guitar of his own, Billie Joe's eyes were firmly set on Gilman Street – the area of town where the musicians hung out and the punk clubs thrived. 'Everything that I have now pretty much branched from that whole scene,' he later recalled.

By comparison, Green Day's bassist Mike Dirnt had a troubled upbringing. Born Michael Pritchard, he was adopted in infancy, as his real mother was addicted to heroin, by a Native American mother and white father. But by the time he was seven years old his adopted parents had separated and, since he chose to live with his foster mother and older sister, he was raised without a father figure.

Billie Joe and Mike attended the same school – Pinole Valley High – in the Bay Area of San Francisco, but they didn't meet each other until the fifth year. Both liked being the centre of attention and the pair clashed when they first met in the high school cafeteria in 1982.

Pinole Valley High was in the centre of the small, hilly town, on the shores of San Pablo Bay in between San Francisco and Oakland. The school's charter claims it 'encourages students to be self-motivated learners and offers a wide variety of options including three academies – Environmental Science, West County Conservatory of the Arts, and Sports and Health.'

BUT MIKE AND BILLIE JOE WEREN'T INTERESTED IN EDUCATIONAL ACADEMIES. THEY WANTED TO PLAY ROCK 'N' ROLL.

BEING PUNK ROCKERS GAVE THEM AN ENERGY — A SENSE OF BELONGING TO AN EXCLUSIVE CLUB. MIKE AND BILLIE JOE WOULD SEE A SIMILAR—LOOKING KID ACROSS THE STREET, WITH THE BLACK TROUSERS, BLACK T—SHIRT, DYED HAIR PERHAPS SOME PIERCINGS, AND THINK 'I BET WE'D BE FRIENDS'.

But Mike and Billie Joe weren't interested in educational academies. They wanted to play rock 'n' roll.

Being punk rockers gave them an energy – a sense of belonging to an exclusive club. Mike and Billie Joe would see a similar-looking kid across the street, with the black trousers, black T-shirt, dyed hair, some piercings, and think 'I bet we'd be friends'.

But back then they'd get harassed for being what the local jocks called 'freaks'. Sometimes, on the street, a car full of them would kerb-crawl Mike and Billie Joe, shouting, 'Hey, freaks, we're gonna kick your ass', and then watch as they scuttled off.

The pair hated going to school in suburbia. They could see the no-hopers a few years above them, leaving school and ending up sitting around doing speed and working in the local burger joint or at a mindless 9-to-5 to fund their habits, instead of going out and really doing what they wanted.

Left to their own devices, Mike and Billie Joe spent most of their free time working on songs together or hanging out at Rod's Hickory Pit where they moonlighted in the kitchens to earn some cash. By the time Mike had turned fifteen he had rented a room with the Armstrong family and had formed a close bond with their son.

In 1987 they recruited a drummer, Al Sobrante (born John Kiftmeyer), a few year's older than Billie Joe and Mike, and the trio started a band which they called Sweet Children, and dived head-first into the northern Californian under-ground punk scene. Billie Joe was on lead vocals and lead guitar, Mike was on bass and backing vocals, and Al provided the beat.

The first Sweet Children gig was in 1988 at Rod's Hickory Pit. Where else? A couple of months later they got a second booking: a high school party with local band the Lookouts in a remote mountain home near Willits, California.

A small rural community 140 miles north of San Francisco, Willits' rolling hills were settled by pioneers back in the 1850s and their picket-fence ranches are still there to this day. At the time of the gig, the town was also home to Tre Cool and Kain Kong of the Lookouts.

Only five people went to the party in the mountains but it didn't put a dampener on proceedings. Plugging their equipment into a clapped-out old generator, Sweet Children played by candlelight as if they were the Rolling Stones at Altamount.

Their focus then, though, was cracking Gilman Street in Berkeley – which was and still is a liberal college town where the pace of life is chilled. Most nights you can catch bands at one of the many venues on Gilman Street. The street starts at the I-80 freeway and heads east through an area of low-cost housing where heavy industry and car shops collide with upcoming businesses. Back in 1989 it was lined with punk clubs and Sweet Children quickly became a staple in a burgeoning scene.

They didn't even get paid in those early days and as they were still too young to drink they were forced to play the all-ages clubs. One of the most famous of these was 924 Gilman. A small membership fee was required before kids could enter this punk oasis. Its goal was straightforward enough: to provide a drug and alcohol-free environment for kids in the Berkeley area. It was run by the Gilman Street Project or Alternative Music Foundation as it was also known, and had fast become an East Bay institution.

924 Gilman wasn't just a breeding ground for Green Day, but later for Sleater-Kinney too – an all-girl group, founded in 1994, inspired largely by Bikini Kill, and a firm part of the mushrooming 'Riot Grrrl' scene.

924 Gilman was also a safe-haven; somewhere parents could be content in the knowledge their kids were okay. A member of the Berkeley Parents Network wrote: 'My daughter's passion is music... the kind that is hard for someone like me to relate to. She went to the Gilman club for the first time this weekend and apparently loved it. It was very intimidating to see the "scene" as I dropped her off but I reminded myself that all those unusual looking folks are people's kids. My daughter also emulates that "look" (the dyed hair, black clothes, piercings) but I figure it is just another stage. Remember when all they wore was Osh Kosh overalls, or pink and purple.'

In 1988, then 17-year-old seniors in High School, Billie Joe, Mike and Al spent two days and what little money they had recording a demo which would later become their debut EP, *1000 hours*.

A copy was sent to Lookout Records, a small indie label that had been based in Berkeley since it was formed in 1988 by Lawrence Livermore, the lead singer of punk band The Lookouts.

From the beginning Lookout had mainly promoted punk bands but gradually expanded to include punk pop, heavy metal and indie.

Livermore was suitably impressed – enough to get the lads to sign a contract and release the disc. Although *1000 hours* was recorded under the name Sweet Children, Billie Joe, Mike and Al had already changed their name to Green Day by the time the record hit the shop shelves a couple of months later.

THE PHRASE 'GREEN DAY' WAS BAY— AREA SLANG FOR HANGING OUT, SMOKING WEED OR GREEN BUD ALL DAY. BILLIE JOE ORIGINALLY WROTE A SONG ENTITLED GREEN DAY ABOUT HIS FIRST EXPERIENCES SMOKING POT BUT THE TRIO THOUGHT IT WAS A BETTER BAND NAME THAN SWEET CHILDREN.

HISTORY WAS ABOUT TO BE MADE.

1000 Hours eventually came out in April 1989. The two-tone, black on green record sleeve was changed at the last minute to reflect the band's name change. On the back of the album was a photo of Billy, Mike and Al standing next to some railings. It contained the title track '1000 Hours', 'Dry Ice', 'Only of You' and 'The One I Want'.

Touring in the early days was a lot of fun. For any band living out of a suitcase, on the open road, miles away from your hometown feels like the pinnacle of success. It taught Green Day to think and play as a band. It also made them tighter than ever and a month after 1,000 Hours was released it was time to tour their debut record. On May 28 Green Day played live at 924 Gilman Street supporting Livermore's band the Lookouts and other local ska-punk act Operation Ivy. Both of these bands were a big influence on Billie Joe, Mike and Al back then.

Operation Ivy's shows were incredibly energetic. Frontman Jesse Michaels was the Ivy's chief songwriter and he belted out his powerful, redolent lyrics in a passionate, throaty voice. Their visit was but a fleeting one, however, the mark they left on the Bay Area music scene with their 2Tone / punk hybrid was indelible. The name Operation Ivy was borrowed from the U.S government's first nuclear weapons test in the 1940s. They formed in 1987 when there was no Lookout Records and the Gilman Street club had only been open a few months, but there was already the beginnings of a scene growing and Operation Ivy played the street's grimy venues as much as they could.

At first only a thousand copies of their debut disc, the Hectic EP, were pressed back in 1988. Today the same record has sold a million copies. Operation Ivy's first full-length LP, *Energy* was recorded in San Francisco the following year but then it was all over. After just two years and couple of hundred frenetic shows, Operation Ivy disbanded leaving the music world a short but sweet taste of their incredible legacy.

The Lookouts formed two years before Operation Ivy and consisted of Lawrence Livermore on guitar and vocals and Kain Kong on bass. Billie Joe and Mike were particularly impressed with their drummer, Tre Cool, who had joined the band at the age of 12. Another band that impressed Billie Joe and Mike was NOFX who were fellow Berkeley natives but who had formed six years before Mike and Billie Joe would put a band together.

NOFX was born in 1983 as a trio consisting of 'Fat' Mike Burkett on vocals, Eric Melvin on bass guitar, and Erik Sandin on drums. They would have more line-up changes than most bands would ever dream of: Sandin left the band two years later to be replaced by Scott Sellers, after which the band relocated to LA. Sellers quit shortly after and his place was taken by another Scott: Scott Aldahl. But he only stuck around for a couple of weeks. Burkett and Melvin managed to persuade their original drummer Erik Sandin to re-join NOFX and the line-up was almost complete.

They steered clear of major record labels and any unwanted commercial exposure, steadfast in their determination to remain an underground punk band – something that would become increasingly difficult as the movement gained in popularity. By 1986, when Dave Allen joined as a new vocalist, They had already recorded a number of albums, EPs and singles. Sadly, Allen died in a car accident not long afterwards leaving Fat Mike to continue singing for the band... if singing was the word. *S&M Airlines*, their first full-length LP, was released on the Epitaph label to which the band is still signed today.

Green Day's Mike graduated from high school in 1990. Meanwhile, Billie Joe dropped out and the pair squatted in a house in nearby Oakland – a more crime-ridden but cheaper alternative to Rodeo, and famous as the hometown of adventure author Jack London.

Green Day recorded another two EPs: *Slappy* which included a cover of the Who's 'My Generation', and a collection of older songs which they called *Sweet Children*. A year later they released *39/Smooth*, their debut album for Lookout, and toured their three-minute punk pop songs across the States, building their fan base from the grass roots up. It was their first national tour.

To this day Lookout Records still sells the LP, claiming...

'GREEN DAY EXPLODES ONTO THE SCENE WITH A BRIGHT—AS—HELL BURST OF POP INSPIRATION. THIS SHIT WILL BLOW YOUR HEAD OFF, AND YOUR HEADLESS CORPSE WILL DANCE NONETHELESS.'

It was a romantic tale – three lower-class lads finding that school could offer them nothing of any particular use, and instead picking up instruments and playing their way out of the mundane and pre-determined future they'd been assigned. But it was also a romantic tale that pre-dated Green Day and which is still re-told by newer bands to this day.

It is also, perhaps, a typically English story: The Beatles, Stones, Kinks and Who, while not all personifying 'from the gutter to glory' story of success, all shared, at least initially, a common dislike of authority – a 'you and me against the world' ethic. Almost 30 years from the '60s, it's obvious that Green Day stood for the same thing.

Their teachers back in Pinole Valley certainly didn't think they would make it. They were just a bunch of slackers; no-hopers who would never taste the American dream without the hard study and ambition to become a lawyer, a doctor or stock-broker. A famous rock 'n' roll band? That certainly didn't happen to kids from Rodeo.

Touring all over the country on a budget, Green Day would sleep on fans' floors to keep the cost down. At one particular gig in Minneapolis in 1990 Billie Joe met Adrienne Nesser. The pair started dating and little did he know it at the time, but four years later Adrienne would become his wife.

In his songwriting Billie Joe gave a nod to everyone from Paul Westerberg to Sugar's Bob Mould, but admitted he was mainly influenced by bands such as the Replacements and Husker Du. Critics that would claim Green Day was trying to sound like the Buzzcocks were duly put back in their place by Mike: 'I hadn't even heard the fucking Buzzcocks when we started.' Truth be told, bands such as the Buzzcocks or the Clash didn't really feature in Mike or Billie Joe's record collections back in 1990.

At the end of a hard tour, Al left Green Day on what was supposed to be a temporary basis to head back to college in California. Billie Joe and Mike, however, wanted to capitalise on the success of the tour and keep their growing – but still relatively niche – fanbase happy. They talked about Tre Cool, the drummer from the Lookouts that they had seen play a number of times and who had impressed them with his fast but accurate technique. Al was a good friend but Green Day was now a serious band and one that couldn't slacken off – not at a time like this.

The Lookouts, meanwhile, had lost their drive. They weren't gigging as much and there were no new records in the pipeline. Tre, now 17 years old and living in the Bay Area, agreed to step in as a stop-gap until Al had made up his mind.

But within a few weeks it became obvious he was exactly the sort of drummer they needed. With Lawrence Livermore's blessing, Green Day would move forward with Tre as their new addition; he would become the band's permanent drummer.

Born Frank Edwin Wright III, Tre had grown up in Willits in the Mendocino mountains and had been Livermore's neighbour. His father was a Vietnam veteran and had built many of the houses in the area, including Livermores. When he was a kid Tre had learned to play the violin but claimed 'no noise came out that sounded good' so he discarded the instrument and turned instead to the drums. His neighbour, Livermore, had a punk band and played drums.

Tre thought he could do the same and told his father he wanted to learn. His dad, in turn, presented his young son with a test. If he passed, he would be eligible for drum lessons.

'IF YOU CAN RUB YOUR STOMACH AND PAT YOUR HEAD AT THE SAME TIME THEN YOU'RE HALF WAY THERE,' HE SAID. TRE THOUGHT HE WAS JOKING BUT HE PLAYED ALONG. 'THERE,' HE SAID. 'IT'S EASY.' BUT THERE WAS MORE. 'OK,' HIS DAD SAID. 'NOW CONTINUE DOING THAT WHILE JUMPING UP AND DOWN ON ONE LEG AND KICKING THE OTHER OUT IN A CIRCLE WHILST REPEATING THE PLEDGE OF ALLEGIANCE.'

TRE DID IT. AND HE WAS ALLOWED TO TAKE UP THE DRUMS.

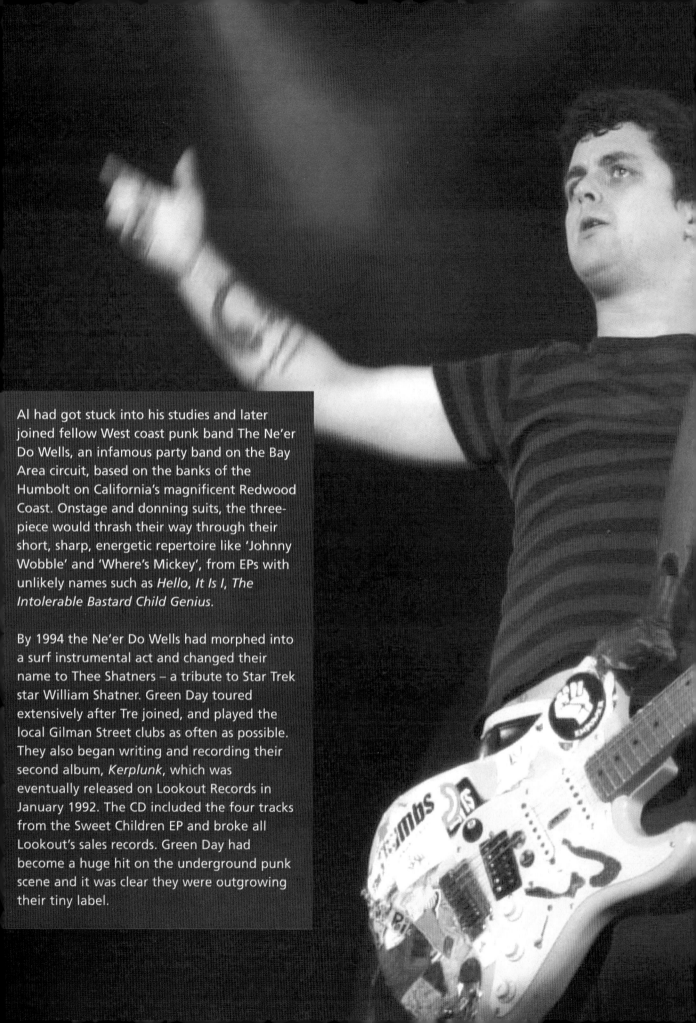

Al had got stuck into his studies and later joined fellow West coast punk band The Ne'er Do Wells, an infamous party band on the Bay Area circuit, based on the banks of the Humbolt on California's magnificent Redwood Coast. Onstage and donning suits, the three-piece would thrash their way through their short, sharp, energetic repertoire like 'Johnny Wobble' and 'Where's Mickey', from EPs with unlikely names such as *Hello, It Is I, The Intolerable Bastard Child Genius*.

By 1994 the Ne'er Do Wells had morphed into a surf instrumental act and changed their name to Thee Shatners – a tribute to Star Trek star William Shatner. Green Day toured extensively after Tre joined, and played the local Gilman Street clubs as often as possible. They also began writing and recording their second album, *Kerplunk*, which was eventually released on Lookout Records in January 1992. The CD included the four tracks from the Sweet Children EP and broke all Lookout's sales records. Green Day had become a huge hit on the underground punk scene and it was clear they were outgrowing their tiny label.

The band toured Kerplunk throughout 1992 and 1993, heading over the pond to the UK and Europe, taking in, Germany, Spain, Italy, Holland, Poland, and the Czech Republic.

While they were climbing the ladder to success, they had to play some of the worst dives on the circuit. Billie Joe later told the *New Musical Express* how the band was almost shot when they reached Germany.

ONE OF THEIR ENTOURAGE HAD JOKINGLY APPROACHED THE FIERCE LOOKING WOMAN ON THE DOOR OF THE CLUB AND ASKED HER 'WHAT WOULD YOU DO IF I PULLED OUT ALL THE MONEY THAT'S IN YOUR POT THERE' THE WOMAN SIMPLY PULLED A GUN OUT OF HER JACKET, POINTED IT AT HIM, THEN TRAINED IT ON BILLIE JOE, MIKE AND TRE AND SAID 'I'D SHOOT YOU.'

Luckily, playing these dives wouldn't last for much longer. They were on their way to bigger and better things.

The band had already garnered a decent following with their EPs and debut LP. Even older punk rock fans who claimed to like nothing but the Pistols, Clash, Ramones and New York Dolls, harboured a secret liking for Green Day's ability to pump out punk rock with a discernable melody.

Their remit was to write simple four-chord wonders that anyone could get 'into'. But Billy Joe sung them with such conviction and, in the words of one reviewer 'adolescent snottiness', that they were also in no danger of ending up in your mum or dad's record collection – the ultimate embarrassment.

One critic pointed out the band had 'really settled into their sound' and in Tre, had added a 'phenomenal rhythm section for Billy Joe's irreverent, snide and sarcastic lyrics.'

Kerplunk contained the original version of 'Welcome To Paradise' and the 'Tre-penned Dominated Love Slave' was a humorous take on the country music that was – and still is – devoured whole by middle America. It also included their searing – and by this time live favourite – cover of The Who's 'My Generation'.

Another critic claimed it was a 'perfect dry run for the band's later assault on the mainstream' and that Billie Joe's 'puppy-dog delivery and eternal switching between snotty humor and sudden sorrow was better than ever.'

Another band of note around the same time was Rancid. Operation Ivy had split up in 1989 and Rancid, formed by guitarist and vocalist Tim Armstrong and bassist Matt Freeman, sprung from its ashes. Armstrong had been dogged by drink and drug problems, and Rancid was intended as more of a project to keep him on the straight and narrow. Their debut single dropped in 1992 on Lookout Records and Billie Joe was asked to join as a second guitarist but he wasn't interested: Green Day were getting somewhere by this point and whilst he was friends with Armstrong and Freeman, he had to decline their offer. Showing that there were no hard feelings he did step in and play live with them on a few occasions, however.

Rancid eventually signed to Epitaph and their first full-length album hit the stores in 1993, which they followed shortly afterwards with a European tour.

In 1993 they released the single 'Radio', co-written by Billie Joe. By now, with their leftist politics, Rancid was one of the hottest bands in the rising punk scene and a serious contender for the crown. In 1995 Rancid released the album *...And Out Come the Wolves* – a pointed metaphor for the A&R scramble to sign the band.

Another Epitaph signing – and another challenger in the punk rock wars – was The Offspring, with their heavy metal-tinged punk. Their self-titled debut was released in 1989 but their huge 1994 release, 'Smash', was their breakthrough. Critics compared the album's first single 'Come Out And Play', to Nirvana, but either way it gave The Offspring the radio play they needed to qualify them for the big league.

Green Day was also inspired (albeit not musically) by bands like Nirvana who had moved seamlessly from the cool indie Sub Pop label, which released their debut LP *Bleach*, to the huge Geffen stable that oversaw the record-breaking 'Nevermind' in 1991. In just two years Nirvana had become god-fathers of the grunge scene but hadn't lost their credibility and hadn't been accused of 'selling out'.

By the same token Green Day's *Kerplunk* was a huge underground success and led to a wave of major label interest. By 1993 the band had sold around 55,000 copies of each of their first two albums – no small feat for a still-underground punk band.

Leaving Lookout on friendly terms, Billie Joe, Mike and Tre eventually signed with Reprise – the label founded by Frank Sinatra and home to Lou Reed and Eric Clapton – which was by now a subsidiary of Warner. With a new record deal must come a new record and Green Day set about writing what would become their breakthrough album.

After signing to Reprise some of their earlier fans accused the boys of selling out. Even after the release of *Kerplunk* and their relentless touring and subsequent increase in popularity, the old Gilman crowd began pointing fingers. Billie Joe was quick to hit back. 'We're just as punk as we used to be,' he said

'WE GOT A LOT OF SHIT FOR BEING SIGNED WITH A MAJOR LABEL BUT WE DIDN'T START THE BAND TO CASH IN A LOT OF MONEY. WHEN WE STARTED OUT, PUNK WAS PROBABLY THE MOST UNPOPULAR MUSIC AROUND.'

WE'RE JUST AS PUNK AS WE USED TO BE...

Black Flag's Henry Rollins too put the boot in. 'He's another bitter old bastard,' Mike would say. 'Basically he's complaining because we've made more money than he has.' Billie Joe was slightly more philosophical.

THERE ARE BANDS THAT WERE MORE INFLUENTIAL TO ME WHO'VE NEVER SEEN THE LIGHT OF DAY. YET EVEN THEY'RE NOT COMPLAINING.' HE TOLD ONE PUNK ROCK MAGAZINE. 'I DIDN'T GET INTO PUNK TO GET FAMOUS.'

However, the trio would return many times to Gilman Street and fans would eagerly await their return each time. The idea that their old fans had deserted them for signing to a major label was, they believed, partly a media invention. 'They like to kind of make more out of something – they want to have some sort of crutch,' Tre said. 'Some sort of way to sell it, a gimmick, you know.'

The lads knew punk had always been there and was there to stay. It didn't matter how the media tried to clean it up or make it more palatable for the mainstream. Billie Joe told one interviewer in 1993 that MTV had 'monopolised the whole thing, inspiring the mainstream to look a little more punk than usual'. This 'punking' of pop music was all a bit contrived, they thought. 'Like the incident where Motley Crue kicked out Vince Neil because they wanted a singer who was more punk,' Billie Joe commented. 'Or how Lars Ulrich shaved his head and grew a goatee.'

Asked whether Green Day would let Reprise 'clean them up' for MTV, Tre was adamant: 'I don't think they'll clean us up because our next record is going to have obscenities in every other song.' But the decision to leave Lookout didn't come easy. Billie Joe, Tre and Mike had been mulling it over for more than a year.

Fed up with dealing with medium size club promoters who often stiffed the band out of money or who would stand by as a gig was cancelled due to a fire marshall declaring it unsafe, Green Day were ready for the stadia gigs.

Some fans bemoaned the fact that kids at their school had started to like Green Day – that the band had become 'trendy' but Mike said that reaction was just selfish. 'We'd played close to 1000 punk shows and it really takes its toll out on you,' he said. 'They had the music when it first came out, so just be glad that you had it years ago.'

In years to come Billie Joe would look back at this moment and say that, for Green Day, signing to a major label had come at the right time. The band had a history, with two full-length albums already released on an indie label, and a decent fanbase.

Ten years on, after Green Day had propelled punk to dizzy mainstream heights, major labels would be scrambling for young punk bands with no pedigree; bands that hadn't even toured, let alone released a single.

Bands need time to develop and they need experience. Something that, by 1994, Green Day had a considerable amount of.

'I DON'T THINK THEY'LL CLEAN US UP BECAUSE OUR NEXT RECORD IS GOING TO HAVE **OBSCENITIES** IN EVERY OTHER SONG.' —TRE

In 1994 Nelson Mandela had become South Africa's first black president; O.J Simpson was arrested for the murder of his wife; Michael Jackson married Lisa Marie Presley; and Kurt Cobain had apparently killed himself with one bullet to the head in his Washington home, joining the long list of rock stars including Jim Morrison, Janis Joplin and Jimi Hendrix, who lived fast and died young.

In the same year Green Day's new album *Dookie* – with its cartoon explosion cover art – sold over eight million copies, bringing their re-working of '70s punk to a new generation. They became overnight stars and *Dookie* catapulted them into the mainstream with catchy workouts like 'Burnout', the stomping 'Longview' and radio-friendly 'When I Come Around'.

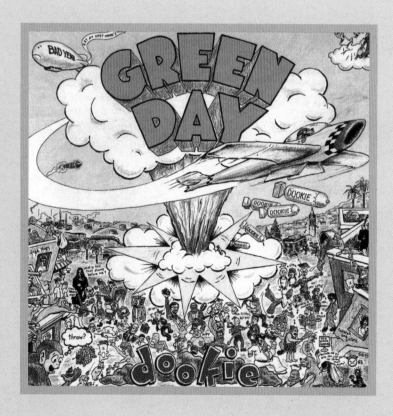

GREEN DAY, ALMOST SINGLE-HANDEDLY, NUKED GRUNGE OVERNIGHT.

Mike thought it was nice that both fans and critics picked up on the difference between Green Day and the grunge bands. He was fond of Nirvana but he knew that Green Day's sound was different; that they were saying something new. He could see a connection between some of the more introspective metal of the Seventies in Grunge – elements of Black Sabbath or Deep Purple. But not with Green Day.

AS USUAL FULL OF CONTRADICTIONS, BILLIE JOE WOULD TELL AN INTERVIEWER HE WAS A 'METALLER'. 'I THINK METALLICA'S MASTER OF PUPPETS IS ONE OF THE BEST METAL RECORDS OF ALL TIME,' HE SAID.

Essentially though, Green Day was and remains a rock n roll band. They may have been extroverts and exhibitionists, writing songs about sex, drugs and growing up but they were ultimately concerned with escaping from the routine and boredom of youth.

Every song on *Dookie* expressed the tedium of adolescence, but was smothered in feisty, mischievous melody.

The *Washington Post* called the band 'sweet-toothed, bubble-gum punks with bad hygiene'.

'They represent the 14-year-old boy in all of us,' another critic wrote. Billie Joe was, he said, '...the class clown, masking his anger and boredom with amiable doofiness and silly faces.'

As for the kids – and later a global audience – we could easily identify with their paeans to teenage alienation and frustration. Millions of copies of *Dookie* were shifted in just a few months thanks to singles 'Welcome to Paradise' and 'Longview', which became MTV staples. By June their first single 'Longview' hit the Top 40 and *Dookie* had been certified gold. Two months later it had been certified platinum and the video for 'Longview' had been nominated for Best Group Video and Best Alternative Video in the MTV Video Music Awards.

One reviewer claimed *Dookie* was '100% pure teenage angst personified in the form of these three dudes named Green Day'. The songs, he said, 'touched on the hopelessness and confusion of coming of age ('Welcome To Paradise', 'Coming Clean') and the hopelessness and confusion of existence ('Longview', 'Sassafras Roots').'

ROLLING STONE'S PAUL CORIO SAID ALTHOUGH PURISTS AND 'MALCONTENT SID VICIOUS NOSTALGICS' WERE BITCHING THAT GREEN DAY WEREN'T ORTHODOX PUNKS IT WAS IMPORTANT TO REMEMBER THAT BEFORE THE SEX PISTOLS AND THE CLASH CAME THE RAMONES — 'WHO IS, BASICALLY, JUST THE BEACH BOYS ULTRALOUD AND PISSED OFF,' HE SAID.

Corio claimed that on Dookie, Green Day 'rendered the spirit of '76 in crunchy pop-guitar hooks, trebly bass and madcap tempos. They're convincing', he said, 'mainly because they've got punk's snotty anti-values down cold: blame, self-pity, arrogant self-hatred, humour, narcissism and fun.' Another said 'Dookie' 'wound up being nearly as revolutionary as 'Nevermind', sending a wave of imitators up the charts and setting the tone for the mainstream rock of the mid-90s… On their first couple records they showed promise but with 'Dookie' they delivered a record that literally found Billie Joe coming into flower as a songwriter.'

There was a world of difference between the sonic quality of Dookie and the albums Green Day had released on Lookout. *39/Smooth* had, after all, cost just $700 to record, and *Kerplunk* $1,500. It was peanuts, and the boys knew the sound had suffered as a result. With *Dookie*, not only were they given money but also more time to pay close attention to what they were doing.

And with an expensive studio, came better equipment. 'The whole album sounds bigger,' Mike told one fanzine. 'That's the main difference between any major label album and an independent album, because the independent albums are recorded on a small budget and they sound transistor to some extent.' ALTERNATIVE ROCK HAD LEGS, AND GENERATION X WAS STILL ANGRY – albeit in a playful way: on stage Billie Joe began to demonstrate his agility: half way through a song he would projectile spit towards the ceiling, catching the remains in his mouth when it descended.

Off-stage, however, the frontman was slightly less flamboyant. Just after the release of *Dookie* he married his girlfriend Adrienne in a civil ceremony in California and shortly afterwards they discovered she was pregnant with their first child. Just as *Dookie* propelled Green Day to superstardom, Billie Joe was going to become a dad.

Mike was quick to correct any journalist who accused the band itself of being Generation X slackers. 'We get plugged with that a lot,' he said. 'But we're not slackers. We just realise that our reality today is a lot harsher… You know, I used to work really hard not to work. It makes sense, considering I know I'll be dead in at least 100 years, so I figured I might as well go out and start looking for something now that's going to make me happy for the rest of my life.'

Billie Joe and Mike were proud of their working-class roots. Their work ethic, they felt, was in-built and they found it offensive if anyone called them slackers. 'We put in some serious fucking hours to be considered slackers,' Mike said. And this was especially poignant for them coming from the notorious 'slacker town' of Berkeley, California. Despite it being the home of one of the most well-respected universities in the nation, it was also popular with hippies and loafers.

If there's one thing Mike, Tre and Billie Joe weren't, it was slackers. Following the release of *Dookie*, the band was thrown head-first into a punishing year-long promotion and touring schedule.

Back in the studio, recording *Dookie*, Billie Joe had played through a Marshall amp that belonged to their producer Rob Cavallo and which he had modified specifically for the sessions in Los Angeles. They called the amp Dookie and later Rancid used the same amp to record their album *...And Out Come The Wolves*.

When Green Day went on tour, Billie Joe wanted a replica made as he liked the sound of the Dookie amp so much. He named it 'Pete'. For the tour Green Day pulled a controversial move; they chose Pansy Division as their opening act. Billed as the first openly gay rock band, Pansy Division formed in San Francisco in 1991. Back then being gay and playing rock n roll - especially of the West Coast punk variety - was unusual. The band was started by guitarist Jon Ginoli and bassist Chris Freeman and it was after signing to Lookout Records that they caught the attention of Billie Joe.

ON STAGE IN CHICAGO DURING THE GREEN DAY SET, KIDS WERE JUMPING OFF A BALCONY AS HIGH AS THE ROOF, ONTO THE CROWD BELOW. MIKE, BILLIE JOE AND TRE WERE PARTICULARLY CONCERNED ON THE DOOKIE TOUR THAT GIRLS IN THE AUDIENCE WERE TAKING THE BRUNT OF THE STAGE—DIVING ON THEIR HEADS AND SHOULDERS. AND IT LOOKED PAINFUL. A FIVE FEET TALL GIRL WEIGHING JUST SIX OR SEVEN STONE TRYING TO CATCH A 12 STONE LUMP JUST WASN'T FAIR

During the Chicago show one guy jumped off the balcony twice while Green Day watched on, helpless. The second time he jumped he knocked himself out cold and the bouncers had to come and remove him.

Aside from the stage-diving reaching dangerous proportions, the tour was a resounding success and Green Day had established themselves as a bona fide contender in the live band stakes. They were certainly not riding on the success of just a couple of singles.

Although the Dookie tour was a success critically and their fans loved it, commercially it was anything but. The band lost around $15,000 on the tour because they insisted on keeping tickets and merchandise cheap. The band was, in effect, paying to play. Something they certainly shouldn't have been doing now they were on a major label. And yet still some of their fans moaned about forking out $10 for a T-shirt.

It was also physically exhausting. Green Day would play ten gigs in a row and then on their one day off they would have to drive several hundred miles to the next venue for the next evening's show.

But the shows were sold out. And after the Dookie tour came the festivals.

Lollapalooza was the brainchild of Jane's Addiction frontman Perry Farrell, and saw bands perform in the dry summer dust and heat of California.

The 'European-style music festival on North American soil' as Farrell put it - part travelling carnival, part celebration of alternative music - was initially intended as a vehicle for Jane's Addiction's final tour. But it fast became an indie music institution.

In 1994 Green Day were on a hefty bill with some impressive rock heavyweights that included the Smashing Pumpkins, The Breeders, Nick Cave and L7. Even the Beastie Boys and George Clinton were thrown in for good measure, ensuring this was an all-encompassing event and there was no rock snobbery going on. Green Day would open for the second half of the tour.

One reviewer claimed they

'POUNCED ON STAGE AND KICKED OFF THE J AM, FUSING PUNK ROCK AND INSULTS.'

Perhaps even more hotly anticipated than Lollapalooza was the return of Woodstock - the legendary 1960s performing arts festival that spawned the phrase: 'if you remember it, you weren't there.'

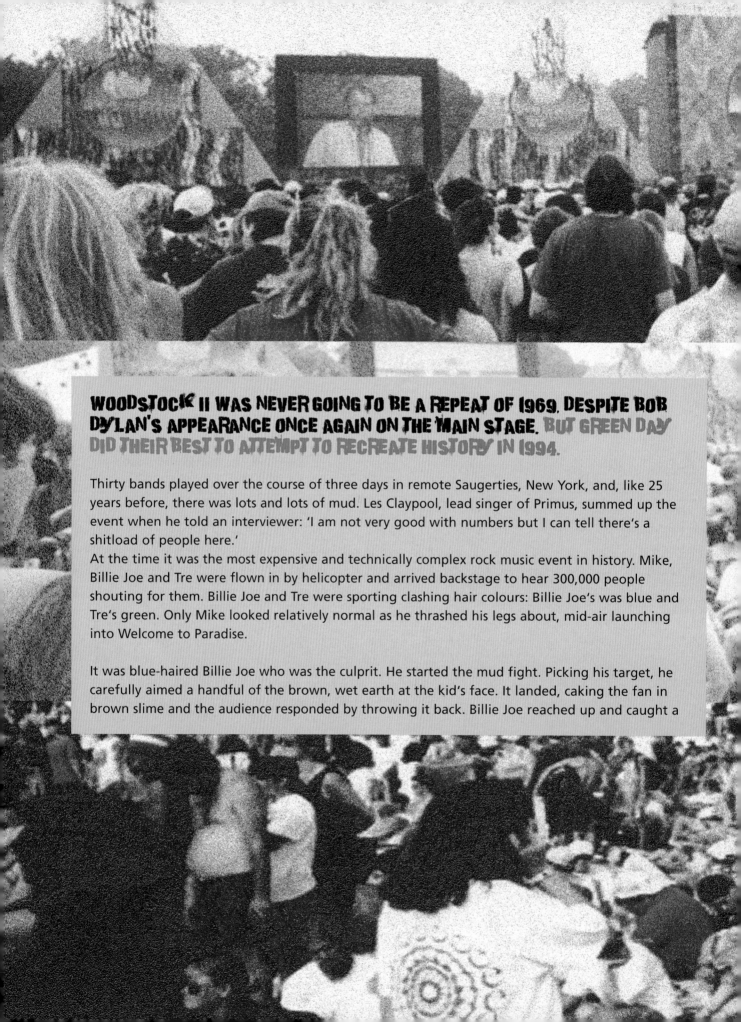

WOODSTOCK II WAS NEVER GOING TO BE A REPEAT OF 1969, DESPITE BOB DYLAN'S APPEARANCE ONCE AGAIN ON THE MAIN STAGE. BUT GREEN DAY DID THEIR BEST TO ATTEMPT TO RECREATE HISTORY IN 1994.

Thirty bands played over the course of three days in remote Saugerties, New York, and, like 25 years before, there was lots and lots of mud. Les Claypool, lead singer of Primus, summed up the event when he told an interviewer: 'I am not very good with numbers but I can tell there's a shitload of people here.'

At the time it was the most expensive and technically complex rock music event in history. Mike, Billie Joe and Tre were flown in by helicopter and arrived backstage to hear 300,000 people shouting for them. Billie Joe and Tre were sporting clashing hair colours: Billie Joe's was blue and Tre's green. Only Mike looked relatively normal as he thrashed his legs about, mid-air launching into Welcome to Paradise.

It was blue-haired Billie Joe who was the culprit. He started the mud fight. Picking his target, he carefully aimed a handful of the brown, wet earth at the kid's face. It landed, caking the fan in brown slime and the audience responded by throwing it back. Billie Joe reached up and caught a

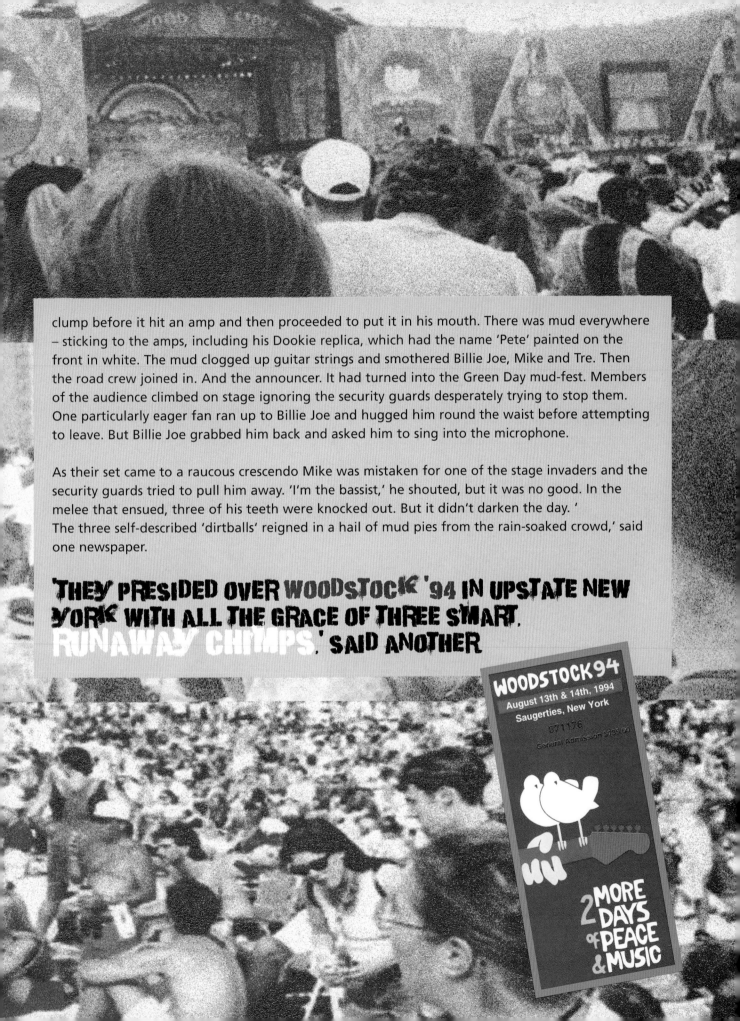

clump before it hit an amp and then proceeded to put it in his mouth. There was mud everywhere – sticking to the amps, including his Dookie replica, which had the name 'Pete' painted on the front in white. The mud clogged up guitar strings and smothered Billie Joe, Mike and Tre. Then the road crew joined in. And the announcer. It had turned into the Green Day mud-fest. Members of the audience climbed on stage ignoring the security guards desperately trying to stop them. One particularly eager fan ran up to Billie Joe and hugged him round the waist before attempting to leave. But Billie Joe grabbed him back and asked him to sing into the microphone.

As their set came to a raucous crescendo Mike was mistaken for one of the stage invaders and the security guards tried to pull him away. 'I'm the bassist,' he shouted, but it was no good. In the melee that ensued, three of his teeth were knocked out. But it didn't darken the day. '
The three self-described 'dirtballs' reigned in a hail of mud pies from the rain-soaked crowd,' said one newspaper.

'THEY PRESIDED OVER WOODSTOCK '94 IN UPSTATE NEW YORK WITH ALL THE GRACE OF THREE SMART, RUNAWAY CHIMPS,' SAID ANOTHER

WOODSTOCK 94
August 13th & 14th, 1994
Saugerties, New York
871176
General Admission $135.00

2 MORE DAYS of PEACE & MUSIC

As for the kids, if they weren't Green Day fans before, they were now. This was what they had been led to believe rock n roll was all about. When their parents harped on about seeing the Stones at Altamount or Hendrix, burning his guitar on stage like an offering to the gods, at the first ever Woodstock, they had tried to imagine a rock 'happening' blowing them away. But it was no use with the insipid, radio-friendly stuff the big stations had been churning out. This was different. They were feeling this. It wasn't just a concert:

IT WAS AN EVENT.

And Green Day were on their side. It really didn't seem like the band was trying to cash in on their new-found fame. Although they graduated quickly from grubby nightclubs to stadiums and hockey rinks, headlining venues they once thought the preserve of people like U2 or Guns n Roses, Green Day kept ticket prices low and sold t-shirts at what seemed like a profit-less price. In keeping with this ethic, less than a month after Woodstock, Billie Joe, Mike and Tre played a free show at the Hatch Shell, Boston, sponsored by a local radio station.

Although the organisers predicted a 'modest'-sized crowd, around 100,000 people turned up in force. It became apparent all too quickly that the security that had been arranged was completely insufficient to control the crowd and the crash barriers came down shortly after the band took to the stage.

THERE WERE FIGHTS WITH LOCAL STATE TROOPERS AND IT LOOKED LIKE THE LIGHTING RIG WAS ABOUT TO COME TUMBLING DOWN SO THE PLUG WAS PULLED ON THE EVENT BEFORE IT WAS OVER. IT WAS MAYHEM AND LOCAL NEWSCASTERS REPORTED THAT EVENING ON THE LATE EDITION THAT OVER SIX PEOPLE HAD BEEN ARRESTED.

But for the band it seemed any news was good news. By March 1995 Green Day were on a roll. They won a Grammy Award for Best Alternative Music Performance for *Dookie* and were nominated for Best New Artist, Best Hard Rock Performance (for 'Longview'), and with 'Basket Case' Best Rock Vocal Performance by a Duo or Group.

BY MAY DOOKIE HAD BEEN CERTIFIED NINE TIMES PLATINUM. IT WAS INCREDIBLE. AND THE THREE LADS FROM THE BAY AREA OF SAN FRANCISCO COULDN'T QUITE BELIEVE WHAT WAS HAPPENING.

Surely they didn't deserve it, but their minds raced back to the hard graft. It was that inspiring work ethic that had driven them and they only had themselves to thank for the position in which they now found themselves.

After Dookie, the ensuing tours and inevitable pandemonium, Mike, Billie Joe and Tre were tired; very tired, and it was time for a well-earned rest. Green Day took time off to 'reassert their roots' according to Mike. This reassertion saw Billie Joe becoming a father to little Joseph Marciano, and Tre Cool, too, settling down; he married long-time

girlfriend Lisea Lyons who was pregnant with a baby girl. The couple called her Ramona – after the Ramones.

It also saw Billie Joe becoming more responsible in his personal life. He found himself with fewer friends back home than he had when he and Mike started Sweet Children all those years ago. But it didn't matter to him. He had a kid now and that was his main focus, along with the band. 'When I get home, I'm a full-time dad and husband,' he said. 'I've got my priorities straight. I'm a father now and I have a certain responsibility. It isn't just my life anymore. I don't want my kid finding bottles in the house or seeing his father completely smashed. I don't want him to get the impression that his father is a drunk. If you have children, you don't want to have drugs and drinks in the house.'

He was also adamant that Joey – as he would be known – would have his own identity and not become known as 'the lead singer of Green Day's son'. He wouldn't be another Rolan Bolan or Julian Lennon. He wanted to let him make his own mistakes and keep him away from the prying eyes of the media.

It was nice for Tre, Mike and Billie Joe to spend time relaxing in California but, as usual, they didn't rest for long.

Green Day was asked to record a song for the soundtrack to a new film directed by Patrick Read Johnson and starring Kathy Bates. Angus was, appropriately, about teen-angst and centred around a 14-year-old fat kid who couldn't get close to the girl he liked at high school. Green Day, now famous for their paeans to teen frustration, were a perfect choice.

The band contributed 'J.A.R' – a tribute they'd written to their friend Jason Andrew Relva who died in a car crash, believed to be a suicide. 'If you could see inside my head / then you would start to understand / the things I value in my heart,' Mike wrote. The song topped the US Modern Rock Charts for a week.

During an interview with *Spin* magazine, Mike rolled up his shirt sleeve and showed the journalist a large tattoo of a snake wrapped around a dagger. The inscription on the metal blade read 'brother'. Jason Relva had the same tattoo and Mike had his done as a tribute to his friend.

'AS GREEN DAY LEARNED,' THE JOUR—
NALIST WROTE IN THE ARTICLE THAT
FOLLOWED, 'LIFE CAN GET
TOO FAST, SPEED OR NO
SPEED.'

Bizarrely the song 'J.A.R' would end up causing Green Day to split with their managers Jeff Saltzman and Elliot Cahn who had taken over at the helm following the release of *Kerplunk*. Cahn and Saltzman were West Coast punk scene stalwarts, also managing The Offspring and starting a record label – 510 – which signed Dance Hall Crashers, a side-project of Rancid's Armstrong and Freeman after Operation Ivy split up.

Rumours proliferated that Cahn and Saltzman had leaked the Green Day single to KROQ – a huge Los Angeles radio station – before its official release as a way of promoting their own fledgling record label. According to the article in *Spin* magazine most industry insiders bought Cahn and Saltzman's side of the story but claimed they 'may not have fulfilled their primary responsibilities as Green Day's managers'.

So Green Day entered the unsteady – and usually inadvisable – realm of 'self-management'. It was, perhaps, a strange decision considering the band was exhausted and finding it increasingly difficult to marry life on the road with a personal life back home. *Spin* called it 'a defiant-some might say naive-attempt to keep their lives and careers their own'

September 1995 saw the video for another single from *Dookie*, 'Basket Case', nominated for nine MTV Video Music Awards including Video of the Year, Best Group Video and Viewer's Choice.

The following month, *Insomniac* was released, astounding some observers by its appearance so soon after *Dookie*. Critics were quick to point out the relatively short gap between Green Day's ground-breaking debut for Reprise, which single-handedly signalled the end for grunge, and the band's hugely anticipated second album.

Although *Insomniac* was seen as something of a rush-release it performed well initially, entering the U.S charts at number two and selling over two million copies by spring 1996. Eventually though, it shifted only a quarter of the units *Dookie* did.

The album dealt largely with Billie Joe's frustrations and perplexity at this rapid ascent to stardom. He was suddenly recognised in the street and found it unnerving. He had money – something he'd never had, especially not in this quantity. And yet he was still frustrated – largely because he didn't feel as if he was allowed to be frustrated any more. People assumed that he had no right to complain about anything now that he was in a top rock band. But he was only human and, well, shit happened. People assumed that because he wasn't working in a 'real job' he should be happy one hundred per cent of the time. They didn't realise just how hard he, Tre and Mike had worked to reach this point.

In some ways *Insomniac* was the antithesis of *Dookie*. Whereas the first album had a catchy, melodic, wild abandon, Insomniac was darker and angrier – more Rage Against the Machine than the Ramones. Billie Joe had even contemplated suicide; he was a man at odds with himself, unsure whether he was doing the right thing in life. Luckily Adrienne was his rock. Suicide, he decided, was too easy. Staying alive was much harder but so much more worthwhile.

The album contained the sinister 'Brain Stew', the Clash-esque 'Brat' and the chugging guitars of 'Panic Song'. But it still managed to be bouncy, energetic and childish. It still bore all the hallmarks of Green Day's angst-ridden immaturity. And the real fans relished it.

But there was no mistaking the album's serious side. 'Geek Stink Breath' tackled the effects of addiction to crystal meth, 'hillbilly crack' or speed as it's more commonly known.

The **CRYSTAL METH** epidemic had swept across the continental United States from the mountain towns in the late 1980s to California in the 1990s, all the way over to the East Coast; its impact was being felt everywhere. Originally it was known to be more of a problem in rural areas, hence its nickname, **HILLBILLY CRACK**, but was fast becoming a major issue in US cities. Serious users would get rotting, brittle teeth that would start to crumble from their mouths after prolonged abuse.

THE DRUG IS MANUFACTURED EASILY IN TINY, DISCREET LABS, COMMONLY PRODUCED USING CAR STARTER FLUID, DRAIN CLEANER AND PAINT REMOVER WITH VARYING AMOUNTS OF LEGAL STIMULANTS SUCH AS CAFFEINE OR EPHEDRINE — EASILY FOUND IN DIET PILLS OR DECONGESTANTS. THE RESULTING YELLOW POWDER CAN BE SMOKED, INJECTED OR SNORTED AND THE RUSH IS DESCRIBED AS SIMILAR TO THE BODY'S OWN ADRENALINE.

Green Day had, in the past, chatted openly of their penchant for drink and drugs, but Geek Stink Breath contains echoes of caution in its vicious portrayal of a man affected by Hillbilly Crack – a warning to friends and loved ones hooked on speed. Billie Joe also admits the song also documented the effect the drug had on himself even though he still confesses to an almost long lost affection for the substance he termed '**ROCKET FUEL**'.

Just before the recording sessions for *Insomniac* had begun, Billie Joe had contacted the company that had manufactured Blue, his beloved Fernandes Stratocaster, to ask whether they could make him a replica to use as a back-up. When the instrument arrived Billie Joe played it endlessly so he could wear it in and get used to its little nuances. But after two weeks the guitar lay in a heap on the floor; the neck had been snapped in two and the strings stuck out all over the place. It just didn't feel right and it certainly couldn't replace Blue.

Insomniac saw a noticeable return to the punk roots from where the band came. It also opened the floodgates for a new wave of punk metal, punk pop and SKA revivalists, cementing Green Day's unquestionable influence on a new generation of musicians.

'WE WERE A COUPLE OF GUYS WITH SHITTY JOBS, PLAYING IN A BAND, HAVING FUN, RECORDING AN ALBUM AND ALL OF A SUDDEN THINGS TOOK OFF,' BILLIE JOE SAID.

'PUNK WENT FROM BEING UNPOPULAR TO ABSOLUTELY POPULAR'

But punks could also be responsible adults too. Slouching on a sofa during one interview, wearing his black sweater, black Dickies, black Converse shoes, and sipping from a hot cup of herbal tea, Billie Joe smiles as he opened his wallet to show the journalist a photo of Adrienne and one of their baby, Joey. 'I may be immature, but I am responsible,' he said.

The journalist noted that, at their core, 'the members of Green Day desire nothing more than to build for themselves, their wives, and their children the kind of family they've hungered for all their lives.'

Being a father was the hardest thing Billie Joe ever had to do, and without Adrienne he is not sure that he would have brought it off. She was a loving wife and a doting mother.

Despite *Insomniac* going double platinum by February 1996 and the band being

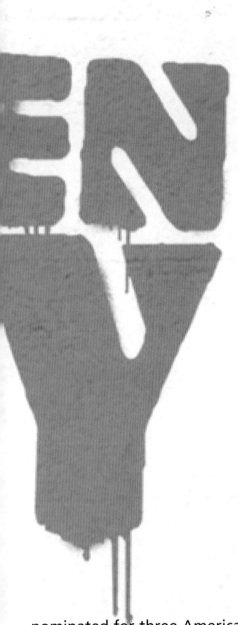

nominated for three American Music Awards for Favourite Artist of the Year, Favourite Heavy Metal/Hard Rock Artist, and Favourite Alternative Artist, there was trouble ahead. A planned European tour was cancelled because Billie Joe, Mike and Tre were exhausted.

Mid-way through, the plug was pulled and the band simply packed up and went home. The press was unanimous in saying it looked as if stardom had just become too much for the three friends from the Bay Area of San Francisco.

THIS WAS, THEY SAID, THE END OF THE ROAD.

But in truth the lads were simply burnt out. They had been touring on and off since they formed the band seven years before and had reached a point where the endless sight of hotel rooms – with their flowery bed quilts, stale cigarette smell and obligatory Bibles – were starting to grate. OK it was a definite upgrade from sleeping on fans' floors, but far more appealing was spending time at home with family or loved ones.

Mike was having panic attacks on a daily basis and any time his tour manager took him to the doctor he was told to take the anti-depressants Prozac or Xanax. He refused to take Prozac and, as it just made him fall asleep, Xanax was no use. Even the enjoyment of being on stage – something that had always been one of the greatest feelings in the world – was beginning to wane, particularly for him and Billie Joe. Mike also began to have chest pains, suddenly dropping to the ground, gasping for air on occasions.

As well as being physically exhausted, the three of them were also bored out of their minds. Being on the road is tedious enough but doing it almost non-stop for seven years was becoming unbearable. It was a seemingly endless chain of driving in the tour bus followed by sound-checking followed by eating, followed by the concert followed by partying, sleeping, driving. It was like a life of *Groundhog Day...* but the everlasting repeats were real, not a movie.

Insomniac, in some ways, was Green Day's way of sticking two fingers up to an industry that was beginning to pigeon-hole them as 'punk pop', or as one journalist called them 'punk rock poster children'. But Billie Joe, Mike and Tre steadfastly refused to be pigeon-holed. Insomniac was proof positive that they could re-invent themselves as harder, more serious artists, but at the same time retain their popularity. It was a strange situation to be in. Although they were now financially secure, the band had to deal with other problems that had come their way.

It was one of the darkest periods in Billie Joe's life and the three friends felt they had no option but to renege on their plans to tour Europe. On top of their general exhaustion, attempting to manage themselves after the spat over the J.A.R single had just caused more stress and Billie Joe and Tre began to get panic attacks, too. The band also felt the shows were suffering musically.

They wanted to concentrate more on their families. Mike wed his long time girlfriend Anastasia in August 1996 and Billie Joe, too, had become a family man. And with that came responsibility. He began to miss his wife and son more and more when Green Day went on the road. He never wanted to do anything besides play in a band and that didn't change but he knew he couldn't take Adrienne and Joey on the road with him.

'JUST BECAUSE WE ALL GOT A BIT OLDER DIDN'T MEAN WE HAD TO BECOME BORING,' HE SAID.

It certainly didn't. On November 21, 1996, Billie Joe was cited for indecent exposure at a Green Day gig in Milwaukee, Wisconsin. He was taken to a police station after the concert, but released after coughing up $141.85 bail money.

Lt. Thomas Christopher of the Milwaukee PD explained what happened, as only a cop could: 'Mr. Armstrong dropped his pants to his knees and exposed his buttocks to the crowd. After the concert, Mr. Armstrong was taken into custody, given a city citation for indecent exposure. He posted a bail and was released.' Mooning is part of Billie Joe's act.

Cancelling the earlier tour hadn't meant the end for Green Day – far from it. They were tired of touring, for sure, but certainly hadn't tired of the only work that ever made them happy. Cancelling the tour would give them time to regenerate, spend some time with their families and come back stronger and better than ever. It was the least they could do for their legions of fans.

Billie Joe, Tre and Mike promised they'd be back with an even better follow-up to the double-Platinum-selling – *Insomniac*. Meantime, the fans still had more Green Day music to devour. In 1996 Reprise also released two EPs: *Bowling Bowling Bowling Parking Parking* – the band's first live recording – and *Foot In Mouth*. The former featured 'Armatage Shanks', 'Brain Stew' and 'Basket Case', among others. Most of the tracks were on *Insomniac* but *Bowling...* arguably showcased the band at their very best: on stage.

Foot In Mouth had live versions of 'Welcome to Paradise', 'Longview' and 'Geek Stink Breath'.

And so 1997 began with Green Day attempting to indulge in some well-earned R-'n'-R back in the Bay Area of San Francisco. Billie Joe could tinker with his prized 1962 Ford Fairlane. Ford originally introduced the car in 1955 but it was re-born in 1962 as Ford's entry into the 'muscle car' market. With its new V8 engine it was lighter than the Galaxie but had the same awesome engine power. It was Billie Joe's pride and joy.

Mike too was a Ford fan, burning round his hometown in an old van. They certainly weren't into the predictable rock-stars' cars.

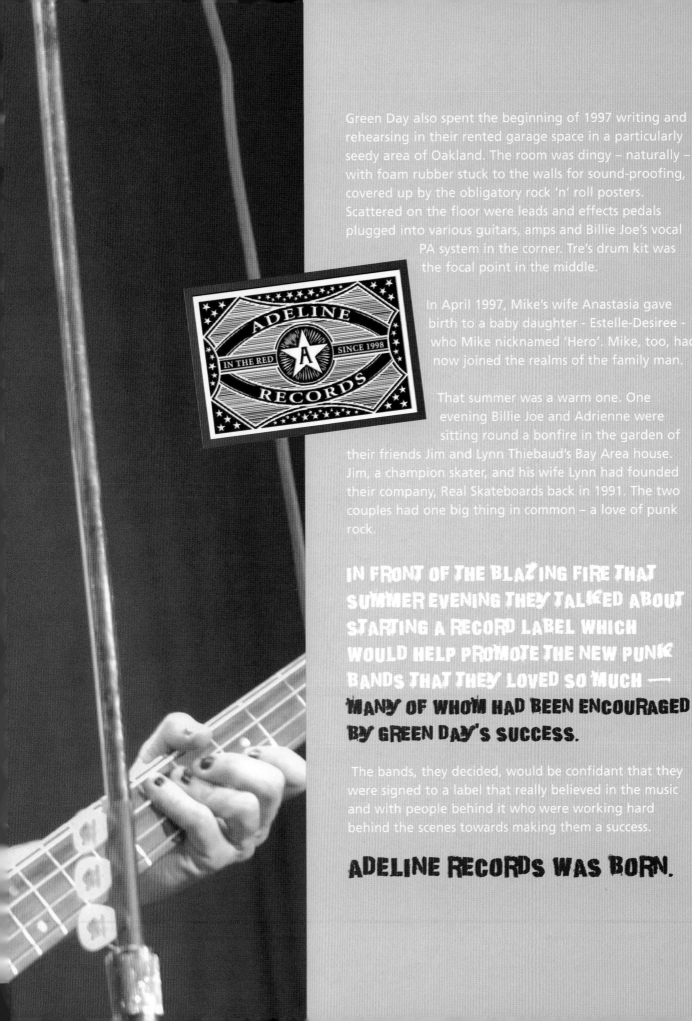

Green Day also spent the beginning of 1997 writing and rehearsing in their rented garage space in a particularly seedy area of Oakland. The room was dingy – naturally – with foam rubber stuck to the walls for sound-proofing, covered up by the obligatory rock 'n' roll posters. Scattered on the floor were leads and effects pedals plugged into various guitars, amps and Billie Joe's vocal PA system in the corner. Tre's drum kit was the focal point in the middle.

In April 1997, Mike's wife Anastasia gave birth to a baby daughter - Estelle-Desiree - who Mike nicknamed 'Hero'. Mike, too, had now joined the realms of the family man.

That summer was a warm one. One evening Billie Joe and Adrienne were sitting round a bonfire in the garden of their friends Jim and Lynn Thiebaud's Bay Area house. Jim, a champion skater, and his wife Lynn had founded their company, Real Skateboards back in 1991. The two couples had one big thing in common – a love of punk rock.

IN FRONT OF THE BLAZING FIRE THAT SUMMER EVENING THEY TALKED ABOUT STARTING A RECORD LABEL WHICH WOULD HELP PROMOTE THE NEW PUNK BANDS THAT THEY LOVED SO MUCH — MANY OF WHOM HAD BEEN ENCOURAGED BY GREEN DAY'S SUCCESS.

The bands, they decided, would be confidant that they were signed to a label that really believed in the music and with people behind it who were working hard behind the scenes towards making them a success.

ADELINE RECORDS WAS BORN.

Bands like Green Day and Rancid had been catapulted to superstardom and the so-called 'Berkeley sound' had become a well-worn moniker. In terms of record sales though, seven years on, this new wave of punk had met with some pretty hardcore rivals in R&B as a genre and individually in heavier bands like Slipknot. Although Green Day was now safely in the lexicon of popular music, hundreds of other younger punk bands struggling to make it in their wake, came up against a music industry moving too fast; unwilling to take a gamble on what they saw as 'last year's scene'.

With Adeline Records there was none of this pressure. Adrienne told a reporter from their local paper in San Francisco:

'WE NEVER REALLY KNOW WHAT WE'RE DOING AND WHAT'S GOING TO HAPPEN NEXT'.

To begin with, Jim wanted to release a record by Bay Area punk band One Man Army - a San Francisco based trio featuring Jack Dalrymple on lead guitar and vocals), Heiko Schrepel on bass and Chip Hanna, formerly of the U.S Bombs, on drums. They were a classic American punk band and had

formed in 1996, playing the local venues in the city. Adeline Records would give them exactly the step up they needed, and the following year the band would see their debut LP, Dead End Stories, hit the record store shelves.

The four friends, Jim, Lynn, Adrienne and Billie Joe, set up a makeshift office in the Thiebaud's dining room and got straight to work. The team began signing other exciting Bay Area punk bands. AFI, Pinhead Gunpowder and the Criminals.

AFI – which stood for 'A Fire Inside' – were a hardcore punk rock band that had formed in 1991 when vocalist Davey Havok, guitarist Markus Stopholese and drummer Adam Carson met at high school. The band hailed from Ukiah, California, 100 miles north of San Francisco on Highway 101, between the Bay Area and Sacramento. Their original bassist was replaced after just a few months by local Geoff Kresge and the bang began playing the local haunts in the Ukiah area. They had disbanded after Havok, Stopholese and Carson went to different colleges and Kresge disappeared to New Jersey to join another band but they got back together during a college vacation and decided to give it a real shot.

Pinhead Gunpowder was a super-group, for want of a better term. It was assembled by Billie Joe and Aaron Cometbus from the band Crimpshrine as a garage side-project but took on a life of its own. They recruited drummer Bill Schneider from Monsula on bass, Jason White from Chino Horde on guitar.

Between 1991 and 1993 Pinhead Gunpowder released a few EPs but in 1994, Lookout Records would re-release all their material on the Jump Salty LP before they moved to Adeline.

The Criminals were an East Bay punk outfit put together by former members of Blatz and The Gr'ups. Burning Flesh & Broken Fingers, their first release on Adeline Records, was produced by Billie Joe.

One critic from the *San Francisco Bay Guardian* called singer Jesse Luscious, a 'Beastie Boys-style contortionist… Ad-Rock mixed with the nerd from the Jerky Boys, lit on fire'. The bands, in turn, began touring relentlessly in order to build on their fanbase and Adeline saw its sales rise.

While working with his wife and friends on the record label, Billie Joe was also writing and recording the new Green Day album with Tre and Mike.

Nimrod, their fifth full-length studio album was released in October 1997 and first single was 'Hitchin' A Ride'. The press was encouraging, widely calling *Nimrod* a return to *Dookie*-era form. The *Montreal Mirror* claimed the 'perfect two minute/three chord aggro-pop songs of dweeby self-deprecation and snotty puppy love will always have a place in the sun, no matter which way the winds of change are blowing.'

In writing *Nimrod*, Billie Joe listened to songs by legendary artists such as Bob Dylan, Tom Waits and Bruce Springsteen. He was intent on keeping one eye on the past and one eye on what was happening in the music scene of the day. He wanted to explore new avenues and experiment with the music. 'Green Day didn't want to record the same album over and over again,' he said.

WITH NIMROD HE WASN'T CONTENT SIMPLY PLAYING POWDER CHORDS. HE WANTED TO EXPERIMENT AND WRITE LEAD BREAKS. BY HIS OWN ADMISSION THIS TOOK PATIENCE AND TIME AS HE WAS MORE OF A RHYTHM THAN A LEAD GUITARIST.

'Mike is a great bass player and Tre's a great drummer,' he told *Guitar World*, 'and it's about letting them play. I'm more of a back-up. We are a very tight unit, and I work with them to enhance the song rather than go off on long, pretentious guitar solos. I'm not a guitar player's guitar player – I'm a songwriter.'

A punishing 15-month world tour was scheduled following the album's release but the pressure of work was too much for Tre and Lisea's relationship to handle and the couple parted... amicably.

Second single 'Good Riddance' (Time of Your Life) climbed the US chart, enjoying regular airplay on MTV. The song was also used in the TV series ER and on the last episode of Seinfeld. But this may have been a bad thing – at least as far as the band was concerned.

Middle-aged businessmen and mothers began humming the song around the house, believing it to be a happy tribute to a loved one. Billie Joe was quick to point out in interviews that its real title was 'Good Riddance', not 'Time of Your Life' and its message was the opposite of the mawkish send-off that middle America wanted to believe.

Many of the people who embraced it and misinterpreted it, he said, were not really part of the band's fan base. But that wasn't to say he didn't like the song he had written. He just wanted it to be understood.

The song was actually written around the time of *Dookie*. The band had always known they had some beautiful ballads in their as yet unreleased repertoire, but wanted to make sure they were released at the right time. None of them, however, could have foreseen that 'Good Riddance' would have ended up as the most-played song of the year. And not just in America – abroad as well.

Unfortunately its huge exposure didn't really aid album sales. *Nimrod* shifted 1.6 million copies in the U.S, slightly more than *Insomniac* but nowhere near the dramatic heights *Dookie* attained.

Billie Joe said that with *Nimrod* the band wanted to record a different album and not just another version of *Insomniac*. If they didn't face that challenge, he claimed, the band would end up 'LIKE SOME OLD PUNK ROCKERS PLAYING THE SAME STUFF OVER AND OVER'.

A fate, he said, which was worse than death.

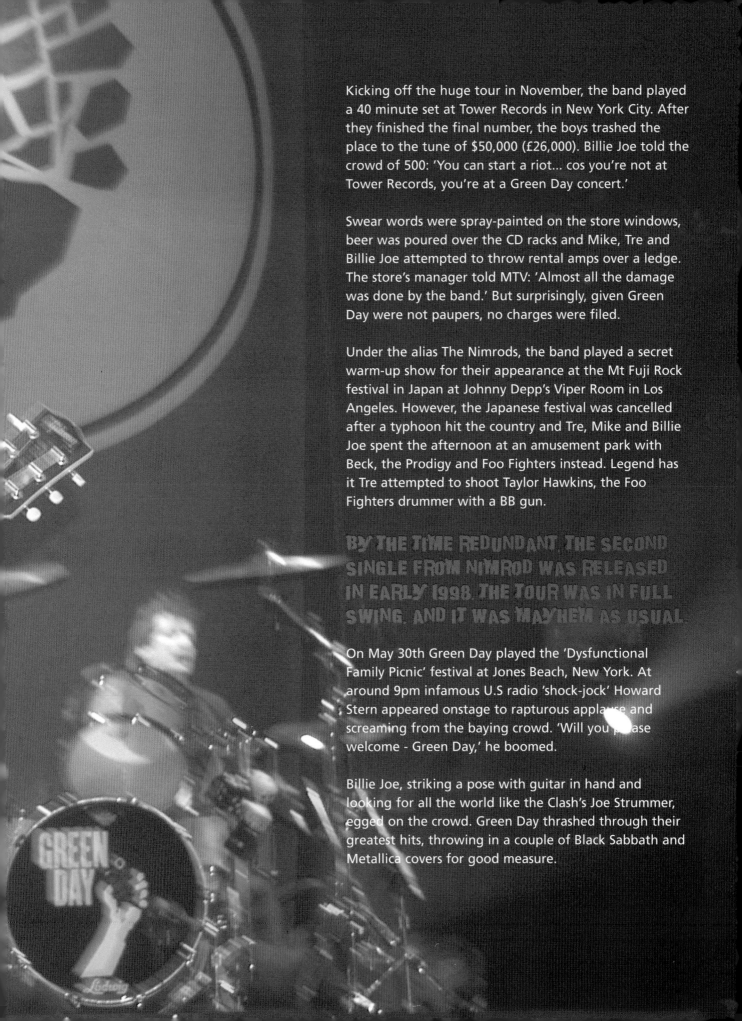

Kicking off the huge tour in November, the band played a 40 minute set at Tower Records in New York City. After they finished the final number, the boys trashed the place to the tune of $50,000 (£26,000). Billie Joe told the crowd of 500: 'You can start a riot... cos you're not at Tower Records, you're at a Green Day concert.'

Swear words were spray-painted on the store windows, beer was poured over the CD racks and Mike, Tre and Billie Joe attempted to throw rental amps over a ledge. The store's manager told MTV: 'Almost all the damage was done by the band.' But surprisingly, given Green Day were not paupers, no charges were filed.

Under the alias The Nimrods, the band played a secret warm-up show for their appearance at the Mt Fuji Rock festival in Japan at Johnny Depp's Viper Room in Los Angeles. However, the Japanese festival was cancelled after a typhoon hit the country and Tre, Mike and Billie Joe spent the afternoon at an amusement park with Beck, the Prodigy and Foo Fighters instead. Legend has it Tre attempted to shoot Taylor Hawkins, the Foo Fighters drummer with a BB gun.

BY THE TIME REDUNDANT, THE SECOND SINGLE FROM NIMROD WAS RELEASED IN EARLY 1998, THE TOUR WAS IN FULL SWING, AND IT WAS MAYHEM AS USUAL.

On May 30th Green Day played the 'Dysfunctional Family Picnic' festival at Jones Beach, New York. At around 9pm infamous U.S radio 'shock-jock' Howard Stern appeared onstage to rapturous applause and screaming from the baying crowd. 'Will you please welcome - Green Day,' he boomed.

Billie Joe, striking a pose with guitar in hand and looking for all the world like the Clash's Joe Strummer, egged on the crowd. Green Day thrashed through their greatest hits, throwing in a couple of Black Sabbath and Metallica covers for good measure.

There was no set list. In fact there had rarely ever been a set list. Green Day would play to the reaction of the crowd, responding to the constant bellowing from the front two or three rows as that was as far back as they could hear. There was a real energy from the crowd this day. Encouraged by the reception the band gathered at the back of the stage and started to set Tre's drum kit on fire. The crowd loved it as the skins burned, sending a plume of black smoke skyward. But it didn't go down well with the backstage security or the attendant paramedics. It was chaos and the emergency services swarmed the stage, including the police. But it was just business as usual for the boys.

The kids loved it and Mike's mind drifted back to a concert a while ago in Rhode Island where kids had also been shouting out their requests as Green Day thrashed out their hits.

A TEENAGER AT THE FRONT WITH GREEN HAIR HAD BEEN SHOUTING 'PLAY KNOWLEDGE, PLAY KNOWLEDGE!' AT THE TOP OF HIS LUNGS AND MIKE HAD MOUTHED THE WORDS 'WE WILL, WE WILL' BUT THE KID COULDN'T HEAR HIM AND BECAME IRATE. 'MAN, FUCK YOU!' HE SHOUTED. 'DID YOU HEAR WHAT I SAID?' MIKE HAD REPLIED, BENDING DOWN AT THE FRONT OF THE STAGE AND STARING THE KID STRAIGHT BETWEEN THE EYES.

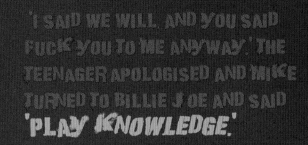

'I SAID WE WILL, AND YOU SAID FUCK YOU TO ME ANYWAY.' THE TEENAGER APOLOGISED AND MIKE TURNED TO BILLIE JOE AND SAID 'PLAY KNOWLEDGE.'

The following month at a festival organised by a Los Angeles radio station, things turned nasty for Green Day. Towards the end of their live set Arion Salazar, the bassist from San Francisco rock band Third Eye Blind, ran on to the stage and wrapped his arms around Mike in a bear-hug. Mike had no idea it was Salazar and reacted by lashing out. In turn, the security guards leapt on stage and manhandled Salazar into the wings.

As Billie Joe grabbed his acoustic guitar to play 'Good Riddance' solo, Mike and Tre left the stage. The official press release stated that 'at this point Mike headed to the Third Eye Blind trailer and got into a tussle with Salazar. Then, suddenly, thinking his hero was being attacked, a Third Eye Blind fan struck Mike over the head with a glass bottle.'

The heavy blow resulted in a fractured skull for Mike but his attacker had disappeared into the crowd and was never found. Green Day was forced to cancel a concert in Sacramento the following night and Salazar later issued a statement apologising for his 'prank'.

'I simply had too much to drink and made a very bad decision,' he said.

Mike was hospitalised briefly but recovered enough to finish the remaining concerts that Green Day had been booked to play.

September 1998 saw the birth of Billie Joe and Adrienne's second child who they named Jakob Danger. It was time, after the long and eventful tour, to take another break.

1999 was a relatively quiet year for the band. In January Green Day was nominated for an American Music Award for Favourite Alternative Artist. The boys released 'Nice Guys Finish Last', recorded for the soundtrack to *Varsity Blues*, starring Jon Voight as a Texas high school football coach.

In June they had a song on the Short Music For Short People LP, issued on Fat Wreck Chords – a San Francisco-based record company specialising in punk rock.

GREEN DAY'S THE BALLAD OF WILHELM FINK WAS ONE OF 101 SHORT, SHARP PUNK SONGS ON AN ALBUM WHICH BOASTED LUMINARIES SUCH AS THE MISFITS, BLACK FLAG, NOFX AND BAD RELIGION.

1999 saw the 'Nimrod' b-side 'Espionage' appear, appropriately, on the soundtrack to the new Austin Powers film, *The Spy Who Shagged Me*. Producer of the film's sound track was Grammy winner Rob Cavallo and, impressed with his input, the band announced he would produce their next album.

Billie Joe also penned the song 'the Angel and the Jerk' with West Coast rocker Penelope Houston. The song featured on the TV show *Friends* and on the 'Friends Again' soundtrack. As with Tre and Lisea two years before, the pressures of being in Green Day had become too much for the marriage of Mike and Anastasia to withstand and towards the end of 1999 they filed for divorce, gaining joint custody of Hero. It was an emotionally draining time, but eventually things would settle down and Mike would learn to live with the new life laid out for him, enjoying spending what time he had with Hero, reading to her and attending Spanish class with her each week.

For their first proper gig in over a year, and their first ever live acoustic performance, Green Day agreed to play Neil Young's Bridge School Benefit concert.

Tre, Mike and Billie Joe respected Neil Young. He was possibly the most influential and distinctive songwriter of his generation and had paved the way for garage bands, grunge bands and country rock acts alike. Together with a friend, Young's wife, Pegi, had founded the Bridge School in 1986 to help severely speech-impaired children in the San Francisco Bay Area. One of Young's children had been born with speech and physical handicaps and the annual Bridge School Benefit Concert had been the primary source of funding for Bridge School for years. Green Day were on the bill with Neil Young himself, Pearl Jam, Billy Corgan and James Iha from the Smashing Pumpkins, The Beach Boys' auteur Brian Wilson and British mod rockers The Who. It was quite a line-up.

DURING THEIR ACOUSTIC PERFORMANCE, TRE, MIKE AND BILLIE JOE GAVE THEIR FIRST EVER RECITAL OF THE TITLE TRACK TO THEIR NEW ALBUM WARNING. IT WAS A SWEET TASTE OF WHAT WAS TO COME.

Despite the troubles in Mike's personal life, the new millennium got off to a good start for Green Day when Espionage was nominated for Best Rock Instrumental Performance at the Grammys in February. On March 4th 2000, Tre Cool married his new girlfriend, Claudia, at a mansion in Brisbane, California and the couple jetted off to Hawaii for a two week honeymoon.

Mike, meanwhile, busied himself with a side-project he had started with some friends from the band Waterdog on the East Coast; a punk rock four-piece known as The Frustrators. And their debut album for Adeline Records was just about to drop.

The Frustrators was never going to be a live project – there were no plans to tour as Mike's Green Day schedule was hectic enough. The music was an eclectic mix of styles, from punk with a country twang, to straight-up rock 'n' roll. And like Green Day, The Frustrators injected everything with a hefty dose of humour.

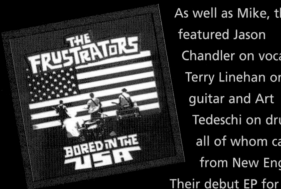

As well as Mike, they featured Jason Chandler on vocals, Terry Linehan on guitar and Art Tedeschi on drums, all of whom came from New England. Their debut EP for Adeline was Bored In The USA – something the record label termed 'a twisting trip through the dusty trails of punk rock and roll. Eight catchy, heart-wrenching songs that cover subjects like alienation, unrequited love for rotting food and midgets used for sport.'

But the 'midgets used for sport' reference was going to land The Frustrators in a whole heap of trouble. The song was called The Great Australian Midget Toss and it first came to widespread public attention when it was aired at an LA Lakers NBA basketball game.

THE LYRICS RANG OUT AROUND THE STAPLES CENTRE STADIUM DURING THE 4TH QUARTER ROUND 'SOME PEOPLE SAY IT'S WRONG / BUT IT'S REALLY FUN / SWING HIM ROUND AND LET HIM GO / LITTLE LIMBS SWING TO AND FRO.'

And it didn't go down well. An organisation called The Little People of America expressed its outrage in the press with its coordinator Casey Hubelbank claiming the song displayed 'insensitivity' to people who suffered from Dwarfism. 'This sends out the wrong message to short-statured individuals and their families,' she said. 'And the fact that it was used as a taunt at a major sporting event only makes it worse.'

Back in the land of Green Day there had been whisperings from some quarters that, arguably, both the new punk movement and Green Day had been much more subversive in their earlier incarnation. 'Remove the communal living, the squalor, the high-octane drugs,' one critic wrote, 'and add in families and a healthy income, and what you have is the suburbanising of – if not the entire movement – then of Green Day themselves,'

But with the band's next album, those voices would be quickly silenced. For whatever Tre, Mike and Billie Joe might have been doing in their personal lives – settling down into some semblance of normality and 'maturity' – their band seemed as edgy and relevant as ever.

Billie Joe was hard at work penning the songs that would form the next album. He told the Los Angeles Times the new record wouldn't contain any songs like 'Good Riddance'. He said he would be 'kidding himself' if he attempted a repeat of the schmaltzy number that he felt had been overused by TV. Looking back at his old lyrics, Billie Joe could see a man full of rage.

'I WAS ANGRY, PESSIMISTIC AND AN EGOMANIAC' he said.

There was an emptiness in his life before but he felt, for once, that he was becoming fulfilled – both personally and as a songwriter. It didn't mean that pent-up anger had dissipated, but that he had learned to channel it better. 'I think it's your own choice if you turn from an angry young man to a bitter, old bastard, or if you stay angry in a good way,' he said. He was convinced his anger was, finally, being channelled in a good way.

He certainly wasn't about to do what he had seen some bands do: portray an angriness for the television cameras in order to project some kind of false persona. Billie Joe certainly wasn't a fake and he couldn't see any reason to suddenly become one. He had also seen songwriters shut themselves off from reality, wallowing in their own emotions but, as he told one interviewer, he didn't want to live in an ivory tower. And so, instead, he chose to live a normal life. Back at home in California he would go out to the shops, drive his car around, go to restaurants with Adrienne. He refused to have that normality taken away.

In July, while the band geared up for the huge Vans Warped Tour – the punk rock parade that rolls into Chicago each summer – LA radio station KROQ informed its listeners:

'ARMSTRONG, DIRNT, AND COOL HAVE BEEN FRANTICALLY DRIVING BACK AND FORTH BETWEEN THREE MAJOR RECORDING STUDIOS AND A REHEARSAL HALL WHERE THEY WERE TRYING TO REMEMBER THE CHORDS TO WELCOME TO PARADISE IN TIME FOR THIS YEAR'S WARPED TOUR WHICH KICKS OFF FRIDAY IN FRESNO, CA.'

Twelve thousand fans turned up for the Vans Warped Tour. More than 25 acts played on five different stages over eight hours but the local *Chicago Tribune* paper said Green Day was the most eagerly anticipated band on the bill.

'They retained their smart-aleck attitude, even while fans pressed into an already overcrowded mosh pit,' the review said. 'Green Day opened the door for punk with a melodic bent to find a larger audience, and many of the bands on this year's Vans Warped bill followed them through it.'

Billie Joe egged on the crowd, looking visibly elated when thousands sang along to 'When I Come Around' and 'Brain Stew'.

Green Day's performance was the climax of the event as thousands of fans gathered to be a part of the event that was unfolding and taste some of that Green Day magic. Billie Joe was up to his old tricks again when one lucky audience member, 'Steven', was asked to join the trio on stage, taking over guitar duties for one number, before stage diving back into the sweating crowd.

News of their incendiary performances had reached Anaheim, California, before the band themselves had. Tre, Mike and Billie Joe arrived on stage on the dot of seven o'clock in the huge parking lot of the Pond - the venue that ice hockey team the Anaheim Ducks played.

Green Day's warm-up consisted of bands like NOFX, ska-metal act The Mighty Mighty Bosstones, Weezer and MxPx.

Whilst Washington descendants MxPx rocked the crowd into a stupor, Billie Joe and Mike were having their pictures taken with fans and signing autographs outside their trailer.

Green Day hit the stage, opening with 'Welcome to Paradise' and closing with 'When I Come Around'. Onstage it was business as usual as the trio bounced around, dodging the now mandatory fireworks.

But while the music on the stage was recognisable, in the merchandise booths something new was happening. The Green Day T-shirts were different, many of them sporting a new logo with the word 'Warning' emblazoned across the front. It was a sign that the new album's arrival was imminent.

Shortly after the Vans Warped Tour, Tre said that he, Mike and Billie Joe knew the *Warning* album so well that they could literally play the entire disc from beginning to end, individually, without the other band members present.

In the studio, recording the 12 songs that would make up *Warning*, things were slightly fraught. Early in the process they decided to get rid of their new producer Scott Litt, who was known for his work with R.E.M, and produce the album themselves. Either way it was the first time that anyone other than Rob Cavallo had produced a Green Day record. Naturally they were on tenderhooks. In writing *Warning*, Billie Joe pushed himself to the limit, exploring styles from artists in his extensive record collection and experimenting with new sounds on his guitar.

Tre described the process as a never-ending repetition of writing, practising, and then playing through the songs, hanging out at home with their families, and then practising again.

'People think we've been off in Hawaii toking grass and shit, but we've been in Oakland the whole time playing our jams,' he said. As if anyone would dare accuse them of tardiness now. *Warning*, was released in October 2000. Sonically, the album was more experimental than anything the band had done before, with noticeably more hard acoustic guitar strumming which Billy Joe said was a nod to Who guitarist Pete Townshend.

MUSICALLY TOO, THEY WANTED TO BRANCH OUT. PUNK HAD ALWAYS BEEN PART OF THEIR MAKE-UP — IT WAS IN THEIR SOUL, BUT THEY DIDN'T WANT TO LIMIT THEIR SOUND.

Reviewers could see what he meant. 'Blood, Sex and Booze', they said, had strong echoes of early Who in its 'garage rock construction'. First single 'Minority' evoked the Kinks' Ray Davies and was given regular airplay on MTV, and 'Hold On', with its guitar and harmonica riff had an air of the Beatles about it. It was, the critics seemed to agree, a musically and lyrically more mature outing than albums past. The *Los Angeles Times* said: 'You can't accuse Green Day's sixth album of being recycled *Dookie* … they've crafted a more coherent, less aggressive but still rebellious collection that also draws on the even older pop traditions.'

Billy Joe told one interviewer: **'OUR LAST RECORDS TALKED ABOUT DRUGS, LONELINESS OR HATE. BUT WITH THIS RECORD THERE'S MORE OF A SENSE OF HOPE.'** While making *Warning* Billy Joe had to get up at seven each morning with Jakob and Joey, take them to school and nursery, and then head back to work with the band. 'I have a lot more lust for life than I had,' he said.

By December *Warning* had been certified gold.

Like 1999, 2001 was a relatively quiet year. Tre's new wife Claudia gave birth to a little boy – Frankito, meaning 'Little Frank' – after Tre's birth name, Frank E. Wright III.

SUNDAY THE CONC

A
SICK OF IT ALL
GOLDFINGER
DILLINGER ESCAPE PLAN
BOUNCING SOULS
HEED & CAMBRIA
NGED SEVENFOLD
GING MOLLY
ER
FIRE
Y PLAN
ED

Shaun of the Dead

Kill Bill Volume 2 + sho

CARLING LEEDS

FRIDAY MAIN STAGE

Compere: Colin Murray

GREEN DAY	21.30 - 23.00
50 CENT	20.00 - 21.00
PLACEBO	18.45 - 19.35
LOSTPROPHETS	17.35 - 18.25
THE STREETS	16.25 - 17.15
DROPKICK MURPHYS	15.20 - 16.05
THE RASMUS	14.25 - 15.05
THRICE	12.45 - 13.15
MINUS	12.00 - 12.30

SATURDAY MAIN STAGE

Compere: Colin Murray

THE DARKNESS	21.30 - 23.00
THE OFFSPRING	19.50 - 21.00
ASH	18.35 - 19.25
THE HIVES	17.30 - 18.15
THE DISTILLERS	16.25 - 17.10
JURASSIC 5	15.20 - 16.05
HUNDRED REASONS	14.20 - 15.00
REEL BIG FISH	13.30 - 14.05
TAKING BACK SUNDAY	12.45 - 13.15
GOLDIE LOOKIN' CHAIN	12.00 - 12.30

SUNDAY MAIN STAGE

Compere: Colin Murray

THE WHITE STRIPES	21.30 - 23.00
MORRISSEY	19.55 - 21.00
THE LIBERTINES	18.40 - 19.30
FRANZ FERDINAND	17.30 - 18.20
THE ROOTS	16.25 - 17.10
NEW YORK DOLLS	15.20 - 16.05
RAZORLIGHT	14.20 - 15.00
THURSDAY	13.30 - 14.05
YOUNG HEART ATTACK	12.45 - 13.15
THE 5.6.7.8's	12.00 - 12.30

MAIN STAGE

THE CARLING

OVER 30 NEW BANDS

KASABIAN, THE SHINS, MARK LANEGAN, MONDO GENERA
THE A'S's, AGENT BLUE, AMPLIFIER, AUTOLUX, BLANC
DEVENDRA BARNHART, BIOS, DO ME BAD THINGS, TH
THE GLITTERATI, INFRASOUND, KAISER CHIEFS,
MR MOJA, MY RED CELL, THE OTHERS, PINK G
ROXY SAINT, SECRET MACHINES, SOM
10,000 THINGS, TV ON

WW

DURING THE SUMMER THE BAND FLEW OVER TO ENGLAND FOR THE REASING AND LEEDS FESTIVALS AND WHILE CROWD SURFERS NEGOTIATED THE HEADS OF THE SWEATING CROWD, TRE, MIKE AND BILLIE JOE LIT A DRUM—KIT BONFIRE. AGAIN.

Around the time of the festivals the band announced it was going to release a 'greatest hits' collection. *International Super Hits*, they said, would feature two new songs – 'Maria' and 'Poprocks & Coke'. 'We've been around for about 12 years and it was just time to put out a collection of all the singles since about '94,' Billy Joe said.

PEOPLE AREN'T ACTUALLY GONNA BUY IT, IT'S JUST GONNA BE THERE AND PEOPLE WILL GO 'WOW, WHAT'S THAT. OH, I ALREADY GOT IT SO FUCK IT',' HE SAID.

In April 2002 Green Day began the huge 'Pop Disaster' tour with Blink-182 and Jimmy Eat World. In the summer they headed over to the UK to play eight shows, including two nights at Wembley, Scotland's T in the Park and Ireland's Witness Festival. By the time they hit London in July they had notched up sales of 23 million albums worldwide and were on fire.

The start of their show at Wembley Arena was heralded by sirens – loud, screeching sirens. Suddenly the band charged onto the stage and launched into their new song 'Maria' accompanied by an arsenal of pyrotechnics.

They circumnavigated their way round hits from all their albums, blasting through 'Longview', 'Welcome to Paradise', 'Brain Stew' and 'Waiting'. They even managed a rather odd cover of Lulu's 'Shout'.

During their performance at Manchester's Move Festival in July, Billie Joe, once again, plucked three fans from the crowd to join him on stage. One of them, Adam McDonnell, was given a guitar to play along with Billie Joe.

Afterwards, before he was ushered off backstage, Adam was given the guitar to keep. 'Practice, cos your sound sucks!' Billie Joe told him.

'It's amazing to have it standing there in my room,' Adam told a reporter for the Virtual Festivals website afterwards. 'I am going to put it into a glass frame on my wall. Afterwards, the band signed it for me, so it's worth even more. And yes we are going to insure it.'

To top off a tumultuous year, Green Day released *Shenanigans* – a collection of cover songs and b-sides. Nestled between their songs 'You Lied' and 'Don't Wanna Fall In Love' was a cover of 'Outsider' – a track made famous by their heroes The Ramones.

The album hit the shelves while the band was still in the UK. The Guardian newspaper reviewed a gig at Old Trafford Cricket Ground in Manchester on July 13th in which Billie Joe sprayed the pogo-ing crowd with water. 'The presence of thousands of green-haired teenage girls inside Old Trafford is a minor victory,' the journalist wrote. 'It is only a couple of years since women were refused entry to the ground's major bar.'

Green Day had become synonymous with a frenetic live show and the press loved them. But by January 2003 Billie Joe's name was in newsprint for a different reason. Early one Sunday morning he was arrested near his home in Berkeley for drink driving. Police said the singer had failed a field sobriety test after being pulled over in his black BMW convertible and had spent a few hours in the county jail before being released on $1,053 (£554) bail.

It was a minor hiccup; the band was going from strength to strength. Green Day's influence on a new generation of bands was cemented later that same year when Skunkaperecords released a Tribute to Green Day called A Different Shade of Green. The album featured Weezer's version of Worry Rock, the Insomniacs covering Minority and Wirebox playing the catchy When I Come Around.

While Green Day were back in the studio writing and rehearsing, a New Wave band appeared on the scene, known as The Network. They almost never played live so no-one knew quite what this five-piece looked like. But they sounded almost identical to Green Day. The frontman, we were told, was called Fink – more than a passing similarity to a comic alter-ego Billie Joe liked to indulge called Wilhelm Fink.

Shortly afterwards, the Web was buzzing with speculation that Green Day had recorded a new album on Billie Joe's Adeline Records called *Money Money 2020*, under the Network pseudonym. The record company's website only further fuelled the gossip by claiming: 'Network are extremely mysterious and never show their faces to humans or cameras.'

UK rock magazine *Kerrang!* reviewed a gig at the Los Angeles Key Club claiming

'IF YOU DIDN'T SEE THEM THAT NIGHT, IT'S UNLIKELY YOU EVER WILL.'

A DVD captured the bizarre show by the Network that night in all its peculiar glory. The band appeared on stage all masked and with each one wearing a more outrageous costume than the last. Red and blue jackets, peculiar headgear, goggles. Even a gas mask. All to stop the world discovering their secret, even though it was one of the worst kept secrets in the world.

THE HIGHLIGHT, KERRANG! SAID, WAS WHEN TRE ABANDONED HIS DRUM KIT TO 'CHARGE AROUND THE STAGE IN A STROBE—LIGHT HAZE, WEARING A BIN—LINER SKIRT AND SINGING THE ULTRA NEW—WAVE 'HUNGRY HUNGRY MODELS'.

If it was a marketing ploy, it worked. Everyone was talking about Green Day. It seemed like the band couldn't get any bigger. But after the Pop Disaster tour the three-piece needed some proper time out to, in Mike's words 're-evaluate ourselves as individuals and as friends.'

Things were not at all well in the personal life of one particular member of the Green Day camp and Tre and Claudia split up after just three years of marriage.

Tre, Billy Joe and Mike's friendship was still tight but they had begun arguing and knew they needed to do something different. Mike even admitted breaking up was an option that they had considered but in the end they had decided they just needed to move forward. And they needed to seriously question which direction Green Day was

heading. Only then could they think about recording the follow-up to *Warning*. And they knew it had to be big.

Not since *Dookie* had they physically dedicated 12 hours a day, five days a week, to sitting down and writing songs with no pressure from outside. In order to maintain their close friendships and retain the whole reason they started the band in the first place, Billie Joe suggested they include weekly 'conversation time' into their writing and recording schedule. 'We bared our souls to one another,' Mike said. There was no-holds-barred conversation and each member admitted they cared for one another. It was important, for without the bond that they had in the beginning, Green Day was pointless.

There were no more tours planned and the record company wasn't on their backs to deliver an album imminently. It was time to contemplate the future. But no one – not even the band – was prepared for what happened next.

They eventually wrote 20 songs for the new album which they recorded at their Berkeley studio but one morning in early 2003 they arrived to discover there had been a break-in and their computer hard drives had been stolen – along with all 20 of the new songs.

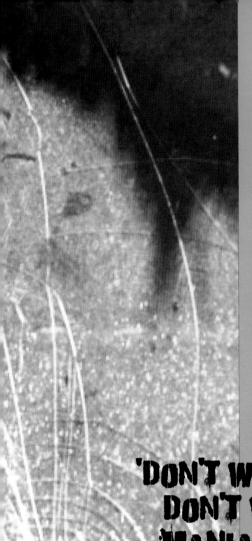

Bizarrely enough, it was to be a blessing in disguise for Mike, Billy Joe and Tre. The lost album could have been salvaged from snippets of songs on laptops, by scrambling round for bits of paper with chord progressions and lyrics penned in black ink, or by tapping into the old grey matter. But the three friends sat down and decided they would start from scratch. They could do better. Much better.

What would transpire was a far cry from the lost recordings. It was March 2003 and the invasion of Iraq had begun with the launch of Operation Iraqi Freedom. The air strikes on Baghdad were crippling and they were played out in all their gory detail on TV screens throughout the world. Billy Joe sat at home during those first few weeks and began writing.

The first song he wrote would become the title track of the new album: *American Idiot* – a contemptuous take on the horrors he was forced to witness.

'DON'T WANT TO BE AN AMERICAN IDIOT / DON'T WANT A NATION UNDER THE NEW MANIA / CAN YOU HEAR THE SOUND OF HYSTERIA' BILLIE JOE YELLS.

At the time the last thing on anyone's mind was a punk opera. But one day Tre and Billie Joe left Mike in the studio alone and when they returned he had written what he termed a 'grandiose vaudeville piece' that sounded like the start of a rock n roll opera.

Billie had some ideas to go with it. A 'concept' album as he put it. Tre did too. And by the end of the week the song Mike had started had topped 10 minutes in length.

Despite its serious content, recording *American Idiot* was a blast. They could see their families and still spend every day in the studio they had rented in the Bay Area. They had demo'ed the songs continuously for months and by the time they were ready to record, the album was pretty much there. It had all been written and the trio were note perfect. All they needed to do was press **RECORD**. They had been so caught up in the production, it didn't seem like work. Tre, Mike and Billie Joe had created a lifestyle out of music and they were enjoying every minute.

The resulting album tackled the media coverage of the war; the actions of the US government; and the seeming lack of concern of the younger generation. Tre told one reporter: 'What I'm angry about is my kids getting sent off to some foreign land to get killed if they bring back the draft.'

MOST OF THE NEW WAVE OF PUNK BANDS WERE LEFT—LEANING ANYWAY BUT BUSH'S WAR MANAGED TO MOBILISE THE MUSICAL TROOPS ONCE MORE. AND THIS TIME, WEANED ON THE CLASH AND THE RAMONES, THEY WERE ANGRY.

Punkvoter was set up by a group of bands, musicians and record labels to educate, register and muster what they termed 'progressive' voters. 'Something needs to be done to unite the youth vote and bring real activism back into our society,' its website ranted. 'Punk rock has always been on the edge and in the forefront of politics. It is time to energise the majority of today's disenfranchised youth movement and punk rockers to make change a reality.'

The brainchild of 'Fat Mike' Burkett of the Californian band NOFX, Punkvoter was, Burkett said, his way of educating the youth about what was really going on in Washington DC and how they could collectively force change. 'This is our chance to be a strong voice against the serious flaws in the current political system,' he said.

Billie Joe too knew that the time was right for Green Day to make some serious social comment; the world from their eyes. They had the benefit of hindsight, of experience. They had the backing of their fans and the support of the music industry. Green Day was huge and the world would listen.

'America is a corporation nowadays and George Bush is a CEO,' Billie Joe said. 'He's not a president. Our album's politically driven. I've always been able to see some kind of political future as far as what goes on in our songs. We're a big-mouth band and that mouth is much bigger when you've got Reprise records behind you.'

Mike was more succinct: 'There's two types of Americans right now: there's them and there's us. And that divides across everything – politically, personally and culturally.'

American Idiot was a concept album – in the same vein as earlier Pink Floyd's *The Wall* – a brave move when it was released in 2004, focusing on the central character, Jesus of Suburbia. It was a public statement – a reaction – to American popular culture. It was overtly political, poignant, ironic, angry, and extremely fresh. For a punk band that had been kicking around since the late 1980s it was incredible but this was the brightest and most appropriate sentiment out there.

Billie Joe was sick of the kids of America worshipping at a shrine of materialism with Los Angeles as its Mecca; its focal point. They were slaves to fashion and slaves to some false concept of youth. 'So damned afraid that one day they might wake up and discover that they've grown old,' Billie Joe said.

'IF BRITNEY SPEARS WOULD PAINT HER ASS GREEN, I'M SURE YOU COULD SPOT GREEN ASSES ALL OVER LA AS SOON AS THE WORD WAS OUT.'

American Idiot entered the U.S sales charts at number one. The *Los Angeles Times* humorously said the record sold so many copies during its first week 'that it's tempting to think some shoppers misread the title and thought the CD was for something in the 'American Idol' series.'

It was incredible to think Green Day could ever top the success of *Dookie* but *American Idiot* gave Tre, Billy Joe and Mike their first ever number one album in the U.S; *Dookie* and *Insomniac* had both reached number two. In the UK the album shot straight to the top, knocking Embrace's *Out Of Nothing* from the number one position. *Rolling Stone* said: 'Against all odds, Green Day have found a way to hit their 30s without either betraying their original spirit or falling on their faces.'

IN APRIL SOMETHING VERY STRANGE HAPPENED. BILLIE JOE DIED.

At least that's what whisperings on the internet would have had the world believe. On the 23rd of that month the web was alive with rumours that the frontman had been killed in a horrific car crash. Fans were mourning throughout the world. Until a statement at Greenday.net announced: 'despite what you may have heard rumoured on the internet, Billie Joe did not recently die in a car accident. Billie Joe, Mike, and Tre are all fine.'

Mike was particularly fine, one website said, after his recent visit to The Wiltern Theatre in Los Angeles to witness the Aussie Invasion tour with Jet, The Vines and The Living End. On the same evening Billie Joe apparently died, Mike went to a concert and even had the audacity, not to mention bad taste, to tell fans on his website: 'The Living End played a smokin' show' and suggest that everyone who had the chance to see them, did.

BUT OF COURSE BILLIE JOE WAS NOT DEAD.

He was gearing up for the Green Day tour. That summer the band played the Reading and Leeds Festivals once more and Billie Joe belted out a mighty and appropriate rendition of Queen's 'We Are The Champions'. The BBC said 'it seemed unimaginable that the same trio of hyperactive upstarts responsible for 1994's *Dookie* could take on stadium rock and get away with it. But, after listening to *American Idiot*, it makes perfect sense for the Californian punks to adopt Freddie Mercury's rally call for their own cause.'

Green Day had taken a big gamble with American Idiot. Would the press – or more importantly their fans – embrace an album that was, essentially, a concept album; a rock opera. It was so far removed from anything they'd done before. But it had that unmistakable Green Day energy. That West Coast magic that only Billie Joe, Tre and Mike could muster.

Their seventh studio album didn't just speak to alienated teenagers; it spoke to everyone. And everyone was sitting up and listening. It was a story, not just of the average Joe Bloggs living under the Bush administration and watching their country booed off the international stage, but the story of Joe Bloggs anywhere, in any country, wanting to understand what was happening in the world. Green Day were saying that not every American was the same. Some of them disagreed with the war. Some of them didn't want to be in the situation in which they found themselves.

It was topical, poetic, and Green Day had just taken a giant stride ahead of every other American punk rock band vying for pole position. The BBC said 'tales of "Jesus of Suburbia", "St. Jimmy" and "Whatsername" are loosely woven together, united by 'rage and love'.'

GREEN DAY HAD COME OF AGE. THE BOY'S HAD MATURED, NOT JUST EMOTIONALLY, BUT PROFESSIONALLY FROM THEIR DOOKIE DAY'S. MUSICALLY THE ALBUM WAS CAREFULLY ARRANGED NO ONE WAS CONTENT ANY MORE WITH A DELUGE OF POWER CHORDS.

One critic claimed they had never sounded so vast. Another said 'Boulevard Of Broken Dream's could easily have belonged in Oasis's back-catalogue, with Billie Joe's vocal prowess coming into its own.

Punk rock had risen above its three or four chord parameter. Live, they had added a keyboard, backup singer, even horns which some said looked like they'd strayed even further from their punk roots. But the critics were unanimous: *American Idiot* sizzled with the band's familiar energy and pop sensibility. It was also their most ambitious work to date.

The Washington post said the album had the 'the playfulness of the Ramones and the pomposity of Queen, the rage of the Sex Pistols and the pop of the Beatles'
In the UK *The Guardian* newspaper said: 'Underneath the body art, the trio are flexing a newly awakened conscience' – referring to the album's message.

Then in December 2004 *American Idiot* was nominated for record of the year, best rock song (for American Idiot) and best rock album at the Grammys.

The album also became one of the top 10 downloads of 2004, seeing the pop single enter a renaissance that was certainly not anticipated. Internet downloads had, for the first time ever, overtaken CD sales.

The British Phonographic Industry told the press that more digital downloads were sold than singles from record shops in the last week of 2004.

The singles chart had been suffering largely from online piracy but, ironically, it was the internet that eventually put paid to the problem. Sites such as Apple's i-tunes with its free software, ease of use, and relatively cheap products, was devoured by a techie-hungry market. It wasn't that they'd stopped listening to music, it was that they were, for a while, moving faster than the industry.

In 2004 Green Day joined U2, Gwen Stefani and Maroon 5 in the best-selling downloads lists. In January 2005, bolstered by the nominations, it was good news again as *American Idiot*, which, by December had fallen out of the U.S top 20, knocked Eminem's *Encore* off the top spot, reclaiming its rightful place at the top of the charts again.

The band headed to the UK as part of their huge world tour, including a show-stopping performance at the Brits where Mike told local radio station XFM: 'We knew this album was either gonna be monumental or career suicide, but we believed in it so we put it out there.'

London's Brixton Academy was hardly ready for the Green Day assault. It was two weeks into the European leg of the tour that had sold 175,000 tickets in less than an hour. While their – by now – trademark pyrotechnics blasted all over the stage, the band thrashed its way through songs from 'American Idiot' and throwing in surprises from their back catalogue for good measure.

'WAKE UP THOSE FUCKIN' REDNECKS IN AMERICA'

Billie Joe shouted to the crowd, referring to his new album's underlying message that not all of America agreed with its president's call to arms, as he launches into the Ramones-esque 'St Jimmy' and almost deafened by screaming and applause.

Then, as had become the norm at a Green Day concert, a few fans were invited on stage to take over on guitar, drums and bass and the small dark-haired girl who had taken Billie Joe's place was given his guitar as a memento.

Crowd surfers hovered over the front few rows; a seething, sweaty mass of bodies bedecked in black clothes and make-up, with the odd green and bleached blonde head bobbing in the dark sea.

AS THE BAND LAUNCHED INTO HOLIDAY, 'A SONG AGAINST ALL GOVERNMENT AUTHORITY', THE CROWD REACHED A PEAK. A CROWD SURFER CLAMBERED ONTO THE STAGE AND ALMOST SLIPPED IN HIS OWN VOMIT.

THE BAND LOOKED ELATED.

The new songs and the old, the *NME* trumpeted, 'hang together as part of one whole, storming rock show. This is masterpiece theatre and tonight's proceedings elevate themselves from the merely magnificent to the historical with the encore "Boulevard Of Broken Dreams".'

Another reviewer wrote, 'While Green Day have matured on album, they're the same animals on stage that they have always been'.

Twenty-four hours after the show Green Day were headlining a sold-out show at Glasgow's SECC arena – the last gig on their biggest tour for 15 years. It was Valentine's Day and love was in the air, although most of it admittedly directed towards the three punk rockers on stage.

10,000 jumping, waving, shouting fans had filled the floor of the SECC to witness the Green Day audio battering while a huge, bleeding heart-shaped hand grenade – the backdrop to the stage antics – hung on the wall behind. Decked out entirely in red and black, Tre, Mike and Billie Joe once again ran on stage to fireworks as images of war flickered on a massive screen behind them.

The fans watched as confetti rained down on the trio and a dancing pink rabbit swigging from a bottle of lager joined them on stage. The music was deafening but there was hardly a face in the huge crowd not singing (or in most cases shouting) along. Although carried along by the strength of the band's songwriting, the real magic, as usual, was in the stage show. And there was no one else who could top them.

From 'American Idiot' Billie Joe et al bounded their way through 'Boulevard of Broken Dreams' and 'Wake Me Up When September Ends', and through their array of hits that had bridged two generations: 'Brainstew', 'Basket Case', 'Welcome to Paradise', 'Pulling Teeth'.

And then it was time for the finale. The band had exited, stage left, for what seemed like an eternity. The crowd were going wild, screaming, stomping their feet in the darkness. The lights were still off so they knew it wasn't quite the end. And anyway, how could it be – Billie Joe still hadn't played 'Good Riddance'. 'Green Day, Green Day, Green Day,' the roar got louder until, suddenly, without fanfare, the band walked back on stage and picked up their instruments.

Tre stood up behind his kit and counted Billie Joe in. 'Well…' the frontman bellowed into the mike. The audience hadn't a clue what came next, '…you know you make me wanna Shout'. It was the punk rock version of Lulu's 'Shout' that they had played at Wembley Arena back in 2002. And once again the fans paid their homage by singing and jumping along in time.

Green Day followed it up with Queen's 'We Are The Champions', paving the way for the moving finale.

Tre and Mike waved their goodbyes to applause but only the die-hard fans knew what was coming next. Billie Joe picked up his acoustic and sat down on a stool that the roadie had placed in front of his lowered microphone. As he plucked and strummed his way through 'Good Riddance' he could hear a few screams from the front of the crowd but most people were silent. The lights had dimmed and the spotlight had fallen on the solitary figure in the middle of the vast stage. It was a fitting end to an incredible tour and this audience, for one, had had the time of their lives.

'MUCH THE SAME AS THEY WERE YEARS AGO WITH THE PROTO— SKATEPUNK CLASSIC BASKETCASE' WROTE THE GLASGOW HERALD. 'ARMSTRONG AND CO ARE IMPOSSIBLE TO DISLIKE'.

The NME summed up the tour: 'We've established that over the last year Green Day have turned out their best work, helped galvanise a generation and been rewarded with the plinth marked "World's most important band".'

Next stop was Los Angeles and the 47th Annual Grammy Awards.

Sporting dyed black hair and thick dark eyeliner, Billie Joe had donned a skinny, black Dior suit for the occasion. Mike and Tre too wore custom-made designer suits. 'Their style has definitely changed,' their stylist admitted to a roving fashion reporter. 'It's still really rock 'n' roll with a punk edge. But they've added some designer pieces.'

The event was to be a belated swan song for Ray Charles who had died aged 73 that June at his home in Los Angeles. His duets album, *Genius Loves Company*, which featured contributions from BB King, Willie Nelson and Bonnie Raitt, earned him six posthumous Grammies to add to his lifetime total of 12, surpassing Santana's *Supernatural* and Michael Jackson's *Thriller*. At the 2005 awards ceremony his gongs included album and record of the year.

In the acceptance speech, on behalf of his late friend, Joe Adams, Ray's manager, said: 'I'll simply say it again, humbly, we accept this wonderful, wonderful award, and we offer humongous thanks to you individually and collectively from the bottom of our hearts.' It was a touching moment and one not lost on any of the other artists in attendance.

Alicia Keys won four Grammys for her album *The Diary of Alicia Keys*. Urban outfits Kanye West and Usher won three trophies each and Maroon Five took the best new artist award.

The ceremony lasted three and a half hours and live performances, thankfully, outnumbered the number of actual gongs presented: Bono joined Stevie Wonder and Alicia Keys for a rendition of the Beatles' hit 'Across the Universe'. Joss Stone sang a tribute to Janis Joplin.

One of the most emotional moments of the ceremony was when the Beach Boys' Brian Wilson, finally, won his first Grammy.

'I waited 42 years for this and it was well worth the wait,' he told the *Los Angeles Times*. 'It represents triumph and achievement in music that I feel that I deserved, and I'm really glad I won.' The *LA Times* reported that the other 'drought' ended as country music singer Loretta Lynn picked up her first awards in 33 years for best country album for the Jack White-produced *Van Lear Rose*. U2 won three Grammys for best rock song, rock performance by a group and short-form music video, all for their hit single 'Vertigo', and taking their total since they formed in 1978, to 17.

Green Day was the only hard rock act nominated in either the best album or best record category. On the day the band won the award for Best Rock Album and as they walked to the stage to accept the gong, Aerosmith's Steven Tyler offered his hand to each of them to congratulate them.

FROM BEHIND THE PODIUM, AND HOLDING HIS GOLDEN TROPHY ALOFT, BILLIE JOE TOLD THE CROWD 'ROCK 'N' ROLL CAN BE DANGEROUS AND FUN AT THE SAME TIME,' AS HE PICKED UP THE BAND'S AWARD FOR BEST ROCK ALBUM. AMERICAN IDIOT AND ALL THEIR HARD WORK HAD FINALLY BEEN VINDICATED.

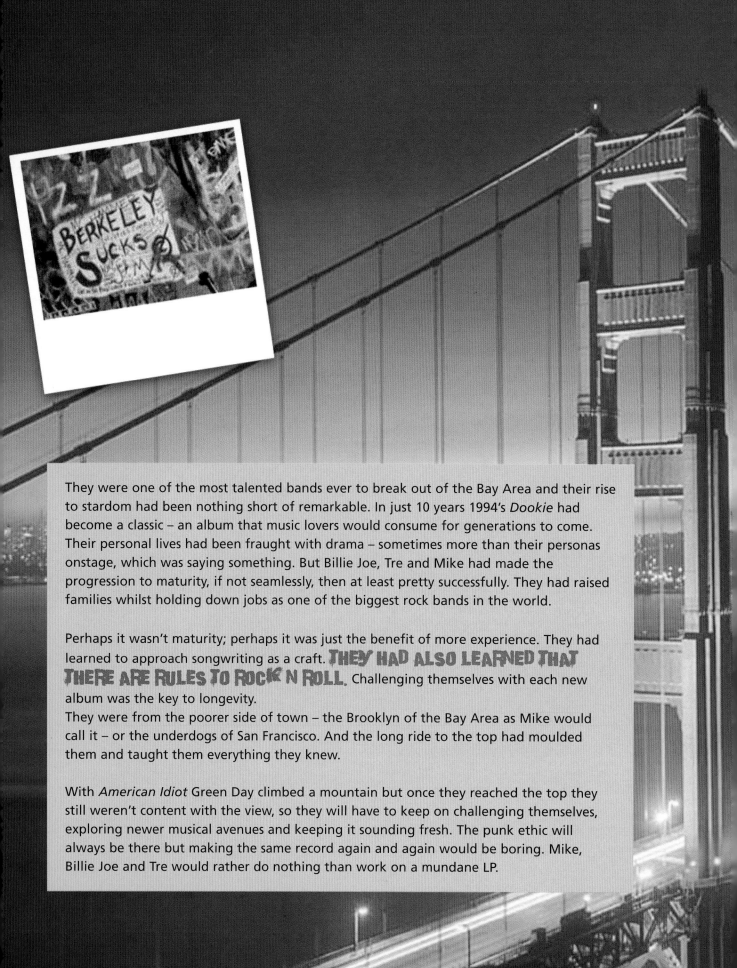

They were one of the most talented bands ever to break out of the Bay Area and their rise to stardom had been nothing short of remarkable. In just 10 years 1994's *Dookie* had become a classic – an album that music lovers would consume for generations to come. Their personal lives had been fraught with drama – sometimes more than their personas onstage, which was saying something. But Billie Joe, Tre and Mike had made the progression to maturity, if not seamlessly, then at least pretty successfully. They had raised families whilst holding down jobs as one of the biggest rock bands in the world.

Perhaps it wasn't maturity; perhaps it was just the benefit of more experience. They had learned to approach songwriting as a craft. **THEY HAD ALSO LEARNED THAT THERE ARE RULES TO ROCK N ROLL.** Challenging themselves with each new album was the key to longevity.
They were from the poorer side of town – the Brooklyn of the Bay Area as Mike would call it – or the underdogs of San Francisco. And the long ride to the top had moulded them and taught them everything they knew.

With *American Idiot* Green Day climbed a mountain but once they reached the top they still weren't content with the view, so they will have to keep on challenging themselves, exploring newer musical avenues and keeping it sounding fresh. The punk ethic will always be there but making the same record again and again would be boring. Mike, Billie Joe and Tre would rather do nothing than work on a mundane LP.

But the trio are realistic. With all careers there are peaks and troughs and it just so happens that at the moment they're at the peak of theirs – something the critics claimed they had already achieved with *Dookie*, and which they couldn't surpass. But they did.

The band knew the new album was good, but none of them thought it could possibly have healing properties. But in March 2005 a nine-year-old Green Day fan from Wales was reported to have emerged from a coma after his mother played American Idiot to him through a set of earphones.

According to the BBC within an hour of hearing the record, little Corey George woke up and began moving his fingers and toes. He had fallen into the unconscious state after being hit by a Sport Utility Vehicle on his birthday and had been unable to speak or move. 'He loves Green Day and is always playing their records,' his father told the reporter. 'The title track we played is his favourite – he listens to it all the time.' While they were putting the finishing touches to a new North American tour, Tre, Mike and Billie Joe found time to send him a box of CDs and T-shirts after hearing the news. Nothing would surprise them any more. It was just another story to add to the increasingly bizarre and wonderful things that had happened over the past sixteen years. Just another incredible addition to the Green Day saga.

BUT THE STORY WAS FAR FROM OVER TO TRE, BILLIE JOE AND MIKE IT ALMOST FELT LIKE IT WAS JUST BEGINNING.

ALL OVER AGAIN.

Revved up and ready to go, the trio had tumbled on to the stage at the ornate Vic theatre in the Central Lake View area of Chicago an hour and a half earlier. They would end the night, appropriately, with a cover of Queen's 'We are the Champions', but before that, as the pyrotechnics died down and a hush fell over the audience, the acoustic intro to new album track 'Wake Me Up When September Ends' kicked in.

'THIS ONE'S FOR JOHNNY RAMONE,' BILLY JOE SAID.

It was a fitting tribute to a band that had lit the flame of punk all those years before. A fitting tribute from a band who had carried that mantle spitting and screaming up to date. A fitting tribute from a band whose journey, despite beginning over a decade and a half ago, was far, far from over.